THE RECORDS OF THE ROYAL AIR FORCE

How to find The Few

PER ARDUA AD ASTRA

CW00820004

Eunice Wilson

Published by the
Federation of Family History Societies
c/o The Benson Room, Birmingham and Midland Institute,
Margaret Street,
Birmingham B3 3BS, England.

First edition 1991
Copyright   Eunice Wilson

ISBN 1-872094-17-1

Cover and title page graphics by Linda Haywood.
Cover illustration by kind permission of Franklin Mint.
Illustration of The Royal Air Force College, Cranwell, from the original by John Bangay. By kind permission of RAF College, Cranwell.
Illustrations on page 39 by kind permission of the Controller of Her Majesty's Stationery Office. Illustrations on pages 42, 47, 48 and 52 by kind permission of the Public Record Office.
Unless otherwise stated all other illustrations by kind permission of 247(F)(China British) Squadron's Association Collection.

Typeset by IMAGO from computer disks prepared by I.S.Swinnerton and Pauline Saul.

ABOUT THE AUTHOR

Eunice Wilson has been a member of the Society of Genealogists for more than twenty five years, via whose shelves, lectures and meetings she learnt the craft of 'tracing your family history'.

Originally a working designer in the shoe industry, she produced *A History of Shoe Fashion* and compiled a shoemakers' index.

The latter has now passed to The Northampton Museum and been amalgamated with their index.

A member of several family history societies, mainly those of Cumbria and Yorkshire in order to develop the study of her own families (Thirkill and Threlkeld), this led to several articles in their journals and consumer magazines. Her father was, among other engineering qualifications, an aeronautical designer during the Second World War. A close friend was killed in the RAF and it was a search into the circumstances of his death which set a second career in motion - free lance researcher into RAF records at the PRO. This, combined with searches for aircraft recovery groups and involvement with the re-creation of an old airfield, Elvington in Yorkshire, as a museum started a long series of research projects. Articles on these subjects have followed; now this guide which we hope will help others to find their own records or those of kin.

Founder Member and Archivist of 247(F)(China British) Squadron Association.

In memory of
920876 Sgt Douglas Charles Ross
of
501 Squadron at Filton and
247 Squadron at Portreath, Cornwall:
a Hurricane night-fighter pilot
killed, aged 20, 11 June 1941
and of no known grave
and of the late
Group Captain P.J.Moore, a Spitfire Pilot

CONTENTS

ACKNOWLEDGEMENTS

Principally, most of the thanks for this book must go to the staff of the Public Record Office at Kew and to experts and friends met there. To ex-Royal Air Force personnel as well as serving members with whom ideas and new lines of discovery have been exchanged I am more than indebted for sharing their knowledge, experience and memories.

Next, the staff of the RAF Museum at Hendon and in particular Peter Murton and Tim Callaway. In the process of working on clients' queries, much has also been learnt and discovered. Among these I must single out Sqn Ldr John Kemp, Battle of Britain pilot, from whom I learnt about radar units and the D Day landings; John Austin for whom I identified the crews of aircraft crashed in training in Cumbria; the dedicated restorers of RAF Elvington (now the Yorkshire Air Museum) - for them I gathered bomber squadrons and the Free French; to James Halley and his book *Squadrons of the RAF*. A wider knowledge I will never meet.

To the pilots and ground support staff of 247 (F)(China British) Squadron in particular, go the greatest thanks of all. Especially to Group Captain Peter O'Brian, Squadron Leader Phil Murton and Jack Meechan of the Squadron's Association Committee, whose patience has been boundless.

For finally getting this book off the ground I would like to thank Pauline Litton for the initial proof reading and Pauline Saul and Iain Swinnerton for their invaluable editorial guidance and expertise.

There are too many others to list personally, but to them also, I am indebted.

Eunice Wilson
Fulham 1991

INTRODUCTION

The Royal Air Force may be the youngest and most recently documented of the armed services but its personnel are not easy to locate unless several basic facts are known. Quite often, through lack of evidence, these are not known and beginners find themselves floundering. This booklet sets out a few finding aids for those interested whether they are searching for their own records or for those of kith and kin.

You may have spent a lot of your adult life in the RAF and still not understand what happens to all the bits of paper which had to be so laboriously filled in. Or you may have spent the war years in it and had 'more important things to do'. That many of these records are now in the Public Record Office at Kew, makes the mysterious passings to and fro of secret documents which did not at the time seem secret (why would the enemy be concerned about a lost gas mask or who won or lost the inter-unit football match?) a lot clearer.

The RAF's records at the PRO are well indexed and relatively easy to follow. As well, they have the advantage of being, in the main, typewritten, so there is little difficulty with handwriting. Its official forms F540 (Operations Record Books - colloquially ORBs or ops books) and F541 (appendices to these) are reasonably consistent whatever squadron or unit is being researched and were much the same in 1939-45 as they are on any modern station today.

F540s were first sent to sector HQ, who in turn sent them to Group HQ, and when they had been collated and analysed there they went on to the Air Ministry. These records/forms are now sent, as squadrons are amalgamated or disbanded, to the Air Historical Branch, **anything less than 30 years old is not yet available**. Some, of course, got lost on the way. Nothing, at the time of writing, is yet available for the post-1958 period.

Not all RAF records are at Kew. Some are still with the Ministry of Defence, as the combination of all three services is now called. Others are at the Air Historical Branch (AHB) of that Ministry. Still more are with the RAF's own Record Office in Gloucestershire which is not open to the public, but whose staff are very helpful in forwarding letters providing not too much is demanded and the service number is given.

The latter cannot be looked at and are divulged only to provable next of kin, although a letter of authorisation from the serviceman him/herself will permit the details to be sent to an agent. Those at Kew, the ones most useful to the researcher, no longer secret and open to all, are found in the AIR class series indexes in the Reference Room, and have been released at one year intervals since 1972 when the Thirty Year Rule lapsed.

The usual procedure is used for locating the piece reference of the place or squadron needed and putting it through the computer to bring material to your desk. Full instructions on how to do this are in the PRO's Leaflet No. 16 *Operational Records of the Royal Air Force* and on the computer terminal itself. As with all family history research, the preliminary homework must be done first. That consists of finding what is known already from letters, diaries, family memory and hearsay, photographs and scrap books. As in other branches of research, one works from the known to the unknown.

Number references given in Part I of this guide are in the class series at the PRO and these are dealt with in more detail in Part II.

Although the 'Brylcreem Boys' are now grandfathers themselves, they are not yet deserving of the term 'ancestor', and those who survived have a wealth of recollection, reluctant though they may be to discuss it. Oral research is therefore valuable at this stage, and it is essential that the results be noted down in detail. To record the names and exploits of those who paid so dearly for our freedom in the years 1939 to 1945 and beyond - the years when the RAF came into its own - is the least we can do. They are not easy to find if we do not, for few of them wish to 'shoot a line' for fear of 'putting up a black'.

Be prepared then, as you read, for stories that will wring your heart, for unless we were part of it, most of us have no idea what lay behind the glamorous image built up about them. These are not remote names in a book written two centuries ago. If he is not your own grandfather, the hero may be the man sitting next to you in the silence of Kew's search room.

To begin, the first requirements are squadron or unit number and the place where stationed or the function of the unit in which he/she served and a date or dates for which a search may be made. Service numbers are not particularly useful at this stage as they are not always entered into the operations books. For writing to official bodies however, they are essential. One of those official bodies might be the RAF's own record office, to whom letters may be addressed as follows:
For officers - RAF PMC (AIR 1B) Room 102, Eastern Avenue, BARNWOOD, Gloucester GL3 E2.
For other ranks - RAF P Man 3c(2), INNSWORTH, Gloucester GL3 E2.

The staff are very efficient and patient and an addressed, stamped envelope may be forwarded to your quarry if he is alive, if not it will be returned. They will not reveal anything to you unless you are provable next of kin, or have a letter of authority to ask.

It is not an easy task to search RAF records anywhere even though they are straightforward. Unlike the army of the past, recruitment, intake and reception depots seemingly did not record names unless there were exceptional circumstances - whether called up or volunteers, they are not listed. They must have been at one time so they may have been victims of the notorious 'weeding'. If it is known where these records are I would welcome help.

Nor are there records which will tell the searcher the home town, description, parents or date of birth. There is little information about pay and movements and for tactical reasons fighter squadrons, for example, were moved about from place to place during the Battle of Britain and beyond, making a man's career difficult to follow. Occasionally you will come across these personal details by accident, eg in the records of evaders/escapers from enemy territory - see W0/208: in exchanges between USA and USAF officers in AIR 20/7630 and sometimes in details of accommodation in the appendix volumes of the station.

Ground crews and administration people were not always moved alongside the squadrons they served. Sometimes you will be lucky and find a whole unit listed when it was moved to another base, complete with Nominal Roll and Movement Orders for the Commanding Officer down, but don't count on it. It is a sad fact that it is easier to find a man who died than one who still lives.

FORM 540: only by close study of the operations books - AIR 27 and 28 - can the details of an individual be found, whether in a front line squadron, maintenance unit or anything else. You will still not find the colour of hair or eyes, how tall he was, or what marks distinguished him from anyone else as you will find in the older army description books. Personal character detail, the facts of his pay and pension or discharge honourable or otherwise, are disclosed only to next of kin. Unless, that is you find a sympathetic writer of the summary at the end of each month, one who cared about people as well as statistics and the weather, both of which were vital.

There are other ways of adding to the front line knowledge of the operations books, though all require patience, time, detective work and imagination. Not for nothing is the Royal Air Force's motto PER ARDUA AD ASTRA - Through Endeavour to the Stars.

....

If I have made errors, they are solely and only mine. If there are things I should know and do not, and have consequently assumed wrongly or omitted, please tell me.

Eunice Wilson
Fulham 1991

247(F)(CHINA BRITISH) SQUADRON

247(F) Squadron received its name of the China British through being subscribed for in 1940 by the British Colony in China. People of other nationalities also donated money and all of them said they would send more. In view of what happened there, it is not surprising no more money came. The donation turned the tide for this squadron and, as a token of gratitude, it became one of the 'named' squadrons created under similar circumstances. Details can be found in the Foreign Office Records - FO 371/25175. Many of these pilots are now members of the Squadron Association, others are accounted for in the Roll of Honour in the parish church at High Ercall, Shropshire.

**247(F)(China British) Squadron
at B78, Eindhoven, November 1944.**

Centre: sitting above the 4 - Sqn Ldr B.G.Stapleton, the CO.
To his left: David Crawford, Jack Meechan, Bill Williams, Michael Shirley.
To his right: ?, Kay the adjutant, Roger Thomas, Bill Orriss.
Centre row (r to l): ?, Ray Stanley, Peter Jones, Fricky Wiersum, ?,?,?,?.
Back row (r to l): Ken Gear, ?,?, Cliff Monk, Bill Brown, ?,?.

Those named have been accounted for, the queries are still unknown.
The CO, centre, Sqn Ldr 'Stap Me' B.G.Stapleton, A South African, was tracked down as a POW in WO 208, which gave his service number, enabling RAF Innsworth to forward a letter.

PART I

GENERAL REVIEW OF THE RECORDS

FOR THE PURPOSES of this guide most of the records mentioned are those freely available at the Public Record Office at Kew, the majority of which come under the class grouping of AIR. These are found on the index shelves of the Reference Room on the first floor. There are three identical sets. One set faces you in green binders, as you come through the door at the top of the stairs. There are two more either side of the door inside the main reference room.

As in most family history searches, the first task, which will lead on to the rest, is to find what documents or letters there are within the family. In the case of an airman (flying, ground or administration), these are likely to be in the form of letters, a log book for aircrew, newspaper cuttings, photographs, medals etc. FIRST then, make a note of any numbers and addresses given, as the initial search into AIR records requires a squadron or unit number or a place.

The average minimum age of aircrew was around 17 or 18, though as in all military accounts there are those who fake their age. The official minimum age for call-up was 17 years 6 months. If you, as searcher, do not know for sure, guess, because the RAF (unless in exceptional circumstances) does not give ages or dates of birth. Personal records such as these are on the man's own personal documents, returned to him, or his next of kin in the event of death, and the originals retained at the RAF Record Office at Barnwood and Innsworth. These cannot be obtained by anyone except the man himself, provable next of kin, or on a letter of authority to an agent from either of these. Occasionally details such as these can be found on POW records or if he evaded capture and made his report on returning to the UK. Sometimes they are included, together with address and next of kin, when there was an exchange of RAF officers with those of the USAAF.

Since many of those who survived are still alive, or members of their families are, age details can be found in the usual way at St Catherine's House, as can their birth and marriage certificates. Death notices however are located in the casualty lists. You will only find a Death Certificate at St Catherine's House, for the 1939-45 period, if the person died in or over the UK. If at sea or overseas there is no certificate.

Unlike the army the RAF seldom moved its personnel en bloc. Unless a whole squadron and its accompanying service echelon was moved abroad, or a very active squadron suffering from combat fatigue was moved to a quieter base, you will find few nominal or muster rolls, and even then not in any familiar or regular form. These movements applied in the main to fighter squadrons rather than those of Bomber Command. You must be prepared to search for your man through various records. Nominal rolls were made and sent to Group HQ, but do not seem to have survived in any regular order at Kew. These will be described later. It is unsatisfactory that members of the WAAF - now WRAF - are not as well recorded as are their male colleagues and counterparts. Perhaps someday someone will undertake this valuable piece of research. As far as possible they are included in this guide.

During an airman's career (commissioned, NCO or other rank), his name and service number was written down many times on many documents (this is true of aircrew most of all, making them easier to find). First when he signed on and next when he reported to an aircrew reception centre such as Uxbridge or Regent's Park. It is difficult to locate these records even if you know when and where, as names are not given. Lists may be held somewhere - possibly the Air Historical Branch? I would

5

appreciate knowing where. Then came posting to an INITIAL TRAINING WING (ITW) often at a southern seaside town where most hotels had been commandeered. These too omit names but the dates will be on his letters enabling you to make a rough guess at the posting-out figures when a course was completed.

Initial training lasted only a few weeks and consisted mainly of square-bashing. The next posting was to an ELEMENTARY FLYING TRAINING SCHOOL - this will be EFTS plus a number. All of these are found by number or place in the AIR 29 index, by unit name or function. For some, if you are lucky, there are group photographs with names. These photocopy fairly well and you will find the names recurring elsewhere. It helps to know what he was being trained for as these group photographs are divided into pilot, observer, gunner and navigator categories. Don't forget that until 1942, Navigators were described as Observers. The O and the single wing of their brevet was replaced in that year with N. Some, of course, continued with the O, and some of the flying schools specialising in navigation training retained the O in their title. Don't let this mislead you, generally speaking it is one and the same.

Pupils at this stage had pilot-under-training (or pilot u/t) (or gunner, navigator, wireless operator u/t etc.) added to their records. All wore a distinctive white flash in their caps or round the band of their peaked caps. Then, basic training completed, to be prepared for the type of aircraft (usually written a/c) in which he was to fly, he was sent to a conversion unit - a CU. This could be operational or not; generally in their last weeks under training novice aircrew went on missions as part of a more experienced crew. If operational, it was fully described as an OTU - OPERATIONAL TRAINING UNIT - not to be confused with an Officers' Training Corps - OTC - found in most boys' schools at the time. Again there may be group photographs with names. These units have numbers, eg 59 OTU was at Crosby on Eden, now Carlisle Airport, and 60 OTU was at High Ercall, Shropshire. Be careful, read right through the operational record - OTUs could change their numbers and stations.

From now on when your man is posted to a squadron from an OTU he can be found in both places by number and name, together with the date of his posting. These postings - in or out - generally come at the end of each monthly summary and are the clues you need. There may be references to his efficiency, how he fared on passing-out tests or if he was held over for another course - not necessarily because he didn't succeed, he could have arrived late, or been sick. In the latter event look in the Station Sick Quarters (SSQ) also at the end of the month. Should anything else happen to him, this also is recorded. Sadly a great many casualties occurred in training at OTU, in which case a full account of the accident whether fatal or not may be found. Unlike army muster rolls of an earlier date, there will be few or no personal details.

The lowest rank of aircrew was not always that of sergeant as it became later. With effect from (usually written w.e.f) 28th May 1940 all aircrew were promoted to sergeant and no-one below this rank could fly. That this was not always adhered to is proved in the casualty lists. This order can be found quoted in 604 Squadron's records in AIR 27/2083.

Aircrew at that time could consist of any rank from LAC - Leading Aircraftman - or cadet u/t upward into the higher commissioned ranks. Of these the captain was always the pilot no matter what his rank or that of the others. This had to be explained often by the Commanding Officer to visiting civilians or allied service people of high rank taken as passengers in service aircraft, who often did not like taking orders from a sergeant.

All aircrew were volunteers. No-one was ever conscripted to fly and members of Auxiliary Squadrons were granted special privileges - no matter what rank, they could not be posted away from their parent base or squadron against their wishes. This roused a great deal of comment and was rescinded later in the war. Even with all this, other ranks require a little more patient research, as do airmen and airwomen other than aircrew.

Most of these are not listed by name, though officers and NCOs on the station's permanent staff may be. Careful perusal of the station's complete but unindexed records are therefore essential - daily routine orders, entertainment and sports lists, gas mask issue and the like may reveal a name or a clue as to where to look next, but there is no regular listing daily as for aircrew. An officer's occupation however, may be located in the AIR FORCE LIST, on the open shelves at the PRO, Kew.

All this information is contained in what are called ORBs - OPERATIONS RECORD BOOKS (FORM 540) - written or typed and still in use today. They are common to operational and non- operational (against the enemy or otherwise) units alike. If an Appendix number or letter is quoted it is worth looking for, though it may not have survived. If in doubt, any serving officer or NCO will be able to explain the use and method of filing. Much, however, depended on the personality of the adjutant or appointed compiling officer. It was not necessary to record any more than the bare facts demanded, and some did just that. Others, perhaps more interested in people or under less stress at the time, added fascinating details of people and things which round out the story. Some could dismiss a whole bomber crew lost on a night op, mentioning only the captain's name. This leads to immense problems. It must be remembered it was very disturbing for a non-flyer to write the details of dead comrades. Sometimes a marriage far from the base will be found, or the birth of a child. There is the occasional flash of humour such as when a 247(F)Squadron pilot was reported as returning from his honeymoon considerably chastened. It is not explained why.

Some squadrons, but very few, kept a personal handwritten diary. This was unofficial but it often helps to identify handwriting. They were not supposed to keep these, nor to take the photographs you will find in them with their own cameras. If you have the luck, as I did, to find one of these for a squadron that broke the rules, there is a treat in store. Here is what cannot be recorded in officialese.

NOMINAL ROLLS. There was only one general MUSTER ROLL made for the RAF and this was when its title changed in 1918. From that date it was no longer the RFC under the command of the army and navy, but a service in its own right with its own high command. The ROLL of 1918 is in AIR 10/323, but it was compiled in numerical order so if you do not know your man's number at that date, you cannot find him. It is, however, being transposed into name order by a private researcher which will help matters considerably. In the meantime, there is no rule for finding NOMINAL ROLLS though they were taken, made and sent to HQ. They give name, rank, number and trade of all the personnel on the station. These are dealt with later.

APPENDIX detail is in the right hand column of the Operations Book and, if found, enlarges the item mentioned. They refer to a separate page in the general records of the station as a whole and can be found in AIR 28 and 29. They have not always survived.

It will be noticed that this guide refers sometimes to the base and sometimes to the station on which was the unit sought. The former began as American usage after 1942, the latter was and still is an RAF description. Both are used because the RAF later adopted the term base so as to be less confusing. You will find both in the records.

There was a regular format for what had to be recorded, but very few units kept to it strictly, so be prepared for variations on the basic theme which seems to have been fairly flexible within the accepted pattern. Occasionally however there is a reprimand from Group HQ above, telling the compiling officer he is not keeping the records as instructed! If you come across this SIGNAL, as they call letters and memos, there will be a noticeable improvement in the detail following.

Though they understood the value and necessity of ground officers, and respected their knowledge, aircrew were sarcastic about their non-flying comrades. You will find them unkindly referred to as Penguins, or 'wingless wonders', their Intelligence Officers called 'Brains' or 'Spy' and some given nicknames which seemed to have no connection with anything. The use of nicknames in the air, though, had a valuable purpose. For security reasons, rank and surnames were not used. The number of the squadron is never mentioned nor from where it came except by recognised code-words. The codes and letters of the day were changed at each briefing. These nicknames tended to linger and were often written into the reports. Thus it is that 'Ginger' Lacey is the name by which the 'ace' is known, and few beyond his family would recognise him as James. Equally 'Paddy' Finucane's name was Brendan, and like many another who fought for the world's freedom in Europe, he never changed his nationality, though Ireland was a neutral country.

To put this knowledge of the RAF's organisation to the test No 11 Fighter Group, HQ at Bentley Priory, Stanmore, covered the London area during the Battle of Britain. It had several main bases - Northolt, Debden, North Weald, Hornchurch, Biggin Hill, Kenley, Tangmere. Each of these had satellite stations and various support units. There is no room to list them here, but they will soon become familiar. Each again kept OPERATIONS RECORD BOOKS (ORBs) duly filled in on Form 540, as still in use today. OPS BOOKS or ORBs, then, logged every operational flight the squadron made for whatever reason, before and after the event. In Bomber Squadrons these include a preliminary Captains' Briefing, listing the pilots of each crew. In Fighter Squadrons this was not necessary, most aircraft being of the single seater type. Non-operational flights are not listed here and must be looked for in the summary, or in the records of the base as a whole in AIR 28 or 29.

In both, the aircraft number, type, its identification letter in order of take-off, the date, target, take-off time and return are listed. In most cases there is a list of bombs and how many were carried, whether there were cameras or leaflets etc on board. At the end of the sortie, when all aircraft had safely returned to base - or not - the landing time and result is entered. For those interested in the geography of the terrain, the route of the bomber is often entered.

At the end of each month, under WORK DONE, the summary details what happened and to whom. This also gives day-to-day background of the actual flying, the weather and anything else relevant. Sometimes it gives casualties, who was reported POW, who went on leave, came back, was sick and anything else the interested compiling officer found useful. At the end of this section, but not always meticulously kept, there are usually two useful lists of names - POSTINGS-IN and POSTINGS-OUT. These are officers and NCOs and in the case of STATION SICK QUARTERS other ranks, nursing orderlies, men and women. They enable you to trace where your man came from and to where he was sent. The SSQ also lists casualties and results, especially for OTUs.

If at this stage you need to know the different heads of departments of the Defence Services, consult the IMPERIAL CALENDAR, a series of red books on the right outside the door of the main Reference Room at Kew. Later in this series, you will see how familiar names in this early period rise in their chosen career. If dates and details of events are needed to check your facts, the ANNUAL REGISTER further along the shelf is useful - eg the death of Italian Marshal Balbo in 1940, whose name gave rise to a descriptive type of RAF operation. Or the 'Great Air Battle over Britain' in that same year, not yet then the **Battle Of Britain.**

THE ROYAL AIR FORCE COLLEGE, CRANWELL

Founded in 1919, the buildings were designed by Sir James Grey- West.
The style bears a similarity to Chelsea Hospital, due to the influence of the then Secretary of
State for Air, Sir Samuel Hoare, (Lord Templewood), M.P.for Chelsea. The building now
contains the College Secretariat and an Officers Mess.

HISTORY AND ORGANISATION

THE RFC AND THE FORMATION OF THE RAF.

It must be repeated that there is no general Muster Roll for the RAF and that the RFC (Royal Flying Corps), from which the RAF was formed, used army ranks - airmen and officers being seconded from different regiments. The creation of the new service produced the only Muster Roll (1918) available, unless there is another one somewhere which has not been released. The existing one, in numerical not alphabetical order, is contained in three fat books at the PRO, Kew in AIR 10/232.

The RFC was formed in 1912. It had military and naval wings, the Central Flying School and the Royal Aeronautical Factory. In 1914 the naval wing became the RNAS (Royal Naval Air Service) and in 1918 the rest, detached from army control, became the RAF. RFC records at the PRO, Kew are in AIR 1 and 2 and in the early operational books of the older squadrons. An RNAS station was established at Cranwell in 1915 but in 1920 Cranwell became the Royal Air Force College - the RAF's equivalent of the Army's Sandhurst and Navy's Dartmouth. If Cranwell is a section of your research project, the class numbers and research references to material at Kew are contained in a book published in 1982 by HMSO *A History Of The Royal Air Force, Cranwell* by Group Captain E B Haslam.

At the outbreak of WWI there were two completely separate services operating their own flying training programmes but coming together to operate the Central Flying School at Upavon. Very soon it became clear that the needs of the Military Wing (RFC) in France were entirely different from requirements at sea, and the RNAS formed at Cranwell. Only when the RFC became the RAF did the new service take over the College.

To search this period of the RAF's infant life, a more detailed knowledge of how the three services were commanded (or a willingness to investigate) may be necessary background reading in order to find in exactly which records the serviceman is to be located. Denis Richards' book *Portal Of Hungerford* should remedy a good deal of this as it also contains lists of PRO class references.

The RAF College at Cranwell became the HQ of No. 11 Group which, as No. 11 Fighter Group, becomes more familiar as the Battle of Britain is studied. In 1918 Cranwell contained :-

HQ No 12 Training Group	Boy's Training Wing
HQ 59 Wing	Physical Training School
Nos 56-57-58	Training Depot Stations

The methods of entry into the College were:-
1. From public or other schools through examination by the Civil Service, by special nomination or recommendation. These regulations were closely coordinated with those governing the entry of Cadets into the colleges of the other services.

2. Entrance from universities and OTCs (Officer Training Corps).

3. Promotion from the ranks but promotion in wartime did not necessitate an officer having to pass through Cranwell as all officers have to do now.

4. Entrance through the Boy Mechanics Training Establishments.

The RAF College was formally opened on 5th February 1920.
There were, as there still are, several time-lengths of contract besides that of the career or permanent commission. These contracts also apply to other ranks, at the end of which they can be renewed or terminated - hence the expression 'time served' or 'time expired' men. These apply to Cranwell as much as to elsewhere. Permanent Officers were also accepted via the OTCs, but few remain, however permanent, until the national retirement age of 65. For the RAF it is usually around the age of 55. This should be borne in mind when searching backwards through your man's career in order to work out dates and ages, (see section on RANK).
OFFICER TRAINING CORPS - an important part of many boys' schools. These initials are not to be confused with the OTUs (OPERATIONAL TRAINING UNITS), the starting point for many an RAF search project. These OTUs include all ranks and trades of aircrew, their chief function being to train flying personnel in the last stages before direct combat duties. They also helped to teach a crew to work together as a team when changing from one type of aircraft to another. In the case of the latter, a CONVERSION UNIT or CU provided the necessary instruction. If a crew was being trained for the really big and heavy bombers which were capable of flying very long distances, they went to an HCU, a HEAVY CONVERSION UNIT. OTCs trained boys whilst still at school for a commission in any of the three services.
Incidentally, the RAF invariably uses the term AIRCRAFT, frequently abbreviated to a/c, not 'planes or machines. Hence those who service them are aircraftmen not aircraftsmen as they are so often mis-termed.
In 1918, the RAF was the world's largest airforce in numerical content - that RFC Muster proves it - and was the first to operate independently of naval and military control. Others followed this pattern later, for example USAAC (US Army Air Corps) was part of the Army which became first the USAAF (US Army Air Force) and finally the USAF (the US Air Force). The army in both countries, however, still retains its air branch, as does the Navy. See section on USAAF, as it was termed towards the end of WWII.
By 1920 the RAF had been reduced to a tenth of its strength, the idea being that it might never be used again in war; 1939 showed how mistaken that was. It still leaves a great many names to be researched and listed!
From 1938 pilots and aircrew entered the RECEPTION UNITS as officer cadets or AC2s. When promoted from this initial rank to commissioned aircrew, the service number changed and the new officer was given a different one - beware of this if searching by number and do not be misled into thinking you have two men. But check it. Numbers dating back to the earliest beginnings can be so checked in THE AIR FORCE LIST, the equivalent of the Army and Navy Lists. This is a series of light blue, hard bound, books which can be found on the open shelves on the first floor at the PRO, Kew and is also available at many reference libraries. By year, it gives an officer's number, rank, date of promotion and seniority, listed under duty or profession, eg pilots are listed under GD (General Duties Branch) which meant flying any kind of aircraft; Medical Officers are in their separate branch, as are Accounts, Dentists etc. in theirs. WAAFs and Princess Mary's Royal Air Force Nursing Service are included as are officers on the Retired List.
The early months of WWII retained some of this original formality but casualties had to be replaced quickly, and not always by airmen who had come up a long and clearly defined training ladder. Promotion could be rapid, training cut to the minimum and the rigid pattern of seniority was not always strictly adhered to. Promotion, however, was still by recommendation as can often be found in the monthly returns in each squadron's ORBs - the OPERATIONS RECORD BOOKS.

But there was still the friendly rivalry between the Auxiliary Squadrons, usually composed of men from a single county or city such as 605 Aux. Squadron whose name was County of Warwick, and between the Volunteer Reserve and the Regulars.

The Air Force Lists contain a great deal of explanation useful to the researcher on the organisation of the RAF. The Retired List in later years is bound in separate volumes, but otherwise is at the back of each year's volume. Beware though if your man is not found in the Retired List. This does not automatically mean he is dead. An officer had to inform the Air Ministry each year before publication. If he did not he was presumed dead but was not necessarily so.

The Retired List is published biennially and covers officers who have retired from permanent commissions, listing them in their substantive ranks. Where courtesy titles are retained in civil life higher than the substantive rank it is shown as 'rtd.'. There is a helpful abbreviations list. Early volumes give the squadrons to which officers were attached, but during the war years, posting could be frequent and this was therefore discontinued. Some RFC and RNAS lists are given in the Navy Lists. At this point there is no harm in stating that the original RAF, between the wars and at the beginning of WWII, was sexist and did not take the inclusion of women in the services seriously - not so true now as women serve in almost every category as they began to do during the war. They are eligible for most posts and trades, commissioned and otherwise, with the exception of combat pilot. See the section on WAAFs.

There **are** women who have qualified for their wings, and there have been women pilots in the RAF in the past. In 1947 the AIR COUNCIL wanted to train up to 200 but only 30 reached the end of the course with the required standard. Several trained at Feltwell after experience with the ATA. In 1990, they were accepted as pilots again.

THE AIR TRANSPORT AUXILIARY (ATA) was not a branch of the RAF and must be looked for in the AVIA class of records. They were civilian pilots and engineers, both men and women, and were insured as service crews were not. They worked closely with FERRY COMMAND, though they were not part of it, and their HQ and Training School were at White Waltham. Many, including husband and wife teams, were killed in crashes due to bad weather conditions in which an RAF pilot would not have been allowed to take off. Details of their casualties can be found in AVIA 15/3619, which gives addresses, ages, experience and parents' or next of kin addresses. From this most information can be gained by cross-referencing with the MU, OTU or squadron to or from which the aircraft was being delivered. For background read Lettice Curtis' well documented book*The Forgotten Pilots*, Nelson and Saunders, Olney, Buckinghamshire, 1971. She learned to fly in 1938 and joined the ATA in 1940.

Example - having found the intriguing detail in AVIA 15 of the death of ATA pilot HRH Prince Chirasakti of Siam who was killed in a Hurricane on 12 September 1942 near Langholme, it was possible to find more in the records of 55 OTU at ANNAN in Scotland, in AIR 29/682.

The men and women of the ATA were often past the aircrew age limit or could not pass the strict medical requirements. Often too they were of overseas origins and might have incurred their own country's anger at joining another country's armed forces. There were Americans who joined for this reason before 1942, volunteering before the USA came into the war.

Fighter & Bomber Command Groups in the British Isles.

There are a few records at the PRO relating to women - see under WAAFs - but aside from this they are not easy to locate whatever the rank. This book makes clear why. Appendix sheets and those pages devoted to Daily Routine Orders are the most likely to yield their names.

THE ORGANISATION OF THE RAF

Researchers into RAF personnel may not need to begin at the top but since a good many of today's 'top brass' began their careers in the lowest ranks, it is as well to be aware of the structure of the service. All three services at one time had their own separate Ministries under a Secretary of State. These are now amalgamated into the Ministry of Defence, a procedure which began to evolve after D Day when intense co-operation was essential. A comprehensive book such as John Terraine's *Right Of The Line* or the three volumes by Dennis Richards and Hilary St George Saunders *The Royal Air Force*, published HMSO, will provide useful background.

THE AIR HISTORICAL BRANCH, MoD, 3-5 Gt.Scotland Yard, London SW1A 2HW holds past records and card indexes of people, squadrons and aircraft as well as a comprehensive library from which a bibliography may be obtained. This department is responsible for what is weeded out and what is released to the PRO. It was also the final repository of those F540s whose compiling officers were often reprimanded for not keeping them accurately as instructed. Since it is not the air force of today which concerns us, the AHB will give fair consideration to justifiable questions if they cannot be answered elsewhere. An appointment is necessary to visit, as it is for NAVAL RECORDS in the Scotland Yard Building in Whitehall though not so in the reading room for the archives of the army above the **Army Museum** in Royal Hospital Road, Chelsea.

Under the Monarch, who holds the rank of Marshal of the Royal Air Force and Air Commodore in Chief of the Auxiliary Air Force (equivalent in peace-time of the Territorial Army or in older terms the Militia), each Command had its own Air Officer Commanding in Chief (generally written AOC, AOCC, or C in C). These Commands were:-

Bomber Command	AIR 14	Reserve Command
Fighter Command	AIR 16	RAF Middle East
Coastal Command	AIR 15	Air Forces in India
Training Command	AIR 32	RAF Palestine & Trans Jordan
Maintenance Command	AIR 17	RAF Iraq
Balloon Command	AIR 13	The 5 above were commanded by
RAF Mediterranean	AIR 23	AOC only in Sept 1939. In Overseas Commands
RAF Aden	AIR 23	
RAF Far East	AIR 23	

The modern RAF has only three Commands - Strike Command, Support Command and RAF Germany - but each covers a wider area than its predecessors, and as there are no heavy bombers now, Strike Command includes both Bomber and Fighter Commands 'as was'. From this it is clear that to simplify your search, it is essential to know in which Command your man served. Knowing the Squadron or unit's number, or its function, helps narrow it down further.

COMMANDS were broken down into GROUPS. For example, Bomber Command consisted of 1,2,3,4,5 & 6 Groups; Fighter Command of 11,12 & 13 Groups initially (10 Group covering the West of England was formed early in 1940); Coastal Command of 15,16,17 & 18 Groups. The others similarly. Any *RAF Hand Book*, especially that of Chaz Bowyer covering 1939-45, Ian Allan 1984, will explain by diagram and detail of areas covered. So does the semi-biography of 'Bomber' Harris, of Bomber Command, Arms and Armour Press, 1984. See BIBLIOGRAPHY.

GROUPS are the HQ of sectional areas of the country (see map).

BOMBER COMMAND

1 Group consisted of 10 Squadrons of Bomber Command, mainly in Lincolnshire and East Anglia centred on Bawtry.

2 Group, 7 Squadrons   3 Group, 8 Squadrons (both north of London).

4 Group, 6 Squadrons   5 Group, 8 Squadrons centred on Grantham.
centred on York
covering Yorkshire and further north.

6 Group, 16 Training Squadrons which supplied the Command's Operational Squadrons.

FIGHTER COMMAND

11 Group consisting of 19 Squadrons responsible for the defence of London and the South East including Kent and Suffolk as far as the Isle Of Wight, where it bordered

10 Group covering the West Country and South Wales.

12 Group of 10 Fighter Squadrons covered the Midlands, Birmingham, Coventry across to Lincolnshire, Norfolk, South Yorkshire, Cheshire, the Wirral and Lancashire. Some of this area was shared with:-

9 Group Midlands and North Wales

13 Group of 7 Fighter Squadrons covered Cumberland, Northumberland, Durham, North Yorkshire, Newcastle upon Tyne.

15 Group had 5 Squadrons of Coastal Command

16 Group, 5 Squadrons   17 Group was Training for the Command

18 Group had 9 Squadrons and so on.

Note that these numbers mesh with each other but do not duplicate. Check for changes of Headquarters and coverage in AIR 25. Sometimes necessity made alterations in the defined parameters.

Each Group was under the command of an officer of Air Rank, that is an Air Commodore or an Air Vice Marshal. Not all squadrons at the beginning of the war were up to strength, especially those of the new 10 GROUP which covered Bristol, Avon, Monmouth, S. Wales, Filton, Colerne, Roborough, Exeter and an area up to and including Oxford.

Pilots were not supposed to trespass on each other's territory, and there was great rivalry between groups, such as between 11 and 12 during the Battle of Britain.

IMPORTANT DATES to remember involving these groups - The Battle of Britain June - September 1940 and the Battle for London 7/8 September to 12/13 November 1940. These were crucial periods during which there were the greatest losses in Fighter Command.

The Squadrons themselves, within each Group, covered a single defined area called a Sector, and were responsible for and answerable to the Sector from which came their Control. Therefore if neither the Squadron nor its Number is known, but a rough idea of the area is, look in AIR 25 for a breakdown of what is within each Group. List all the squadrons it contains and go through them - a tedious method, but there is no other.

SQUADRONS

Squadron numbers, their area and dates, can be checked in James Halley's *Squadrons Of The RAF* and the other two books on the PRO's open shelves covering *Fighter Squadrons Of The RAF* and *Bomber Squadrons Of The RAF*. By finding the date, type of aircraft and the place, isolate the most likely squadrons and check them in AIR 27.

Depending on need and function, a FIGHTER SQUADRON could consist of anything between 12 and 24 aircraft, each holding one or two men. Spitfires and Hurricanes were single seaters; Beaufighters and Mosquitos held two and fighter bombers like Blenheims, three. Any good book on the aircraft type will explain and often give names, as in *Mosquito Squadrons Of The RAF* by Chaz Bowyer, Ian Allan, 1984, which lists squadron numbers and names of pilots. After "scrambling", they operated on their own in combat until the leader recalled them or lack of fuel demanded an early return, or in groups on convoy patrol duties, or they went as protective escorts for bombers. The comprehensive *Typhoon And Tempest Story* by Chris Thomas and Christopher Shores, Arms and Armour Press, 1987, gives pilots' names, squadrons, aircraft numbers and the fate of both. There are similar books for other types.

BOMBER SQUADRONS increased in numbers as the war progressed, as did the established number of aircraft in each from a peacetime 12 to 24. The former were twin engined machines which carried crews of four or five, while the heavier four-engine types could carry seven or eight, and flying boats even more - pilot, navigator, flight engineer, wireless operator (w/op), mid upper gunner (mug), bomb aimer and rear gunner, usually in this order. The rear gunner was "tail-end-Charlie" but this term was also applied to the aircraft last in line. In fighter squadrons this latter role was the 'weaver', sometimes there were two taking turns each side to protect the rest. In bombers, one of the gunners, not the tail gunner, was often also the w/op and thus written wop/ag.

17

THE BADGE OF 247(F)(CHINA BRITISH) SQUADRON

Badge	-	in front of a bezant, a demi-lion erased and crowned holding in the paws a scroll inscribed with the Chinese characters 'Chu Feng'.
Motto	-	Rise from the East.
Name	-	China British
Meaning	-	The bezant and the lion are from Devon and Cornwall where the squadron was born. Originally a fighter flight of 152 Squadron, it became a numbered and named squadron in its own right. Chu Feng means 'a powerful wind from the East' since they flew Hurricanes. Chu Feng became a common signing off phrase for pilots and is still used today to end a letter.

COASTAL COMMAND's larger aircraft crews, in Liberators or Sunderland and Catalina flying boats, were trained at HCU's and were in smaller squadrons but each could carry a crew of ten men or more. Often these large machines had 'spare' men to cover in case of fatigue on their long patrols of sixteen to eighteen hours. In all the big machines there were often two pilots, one who had completed one tour and was experienced, and a new 'fresher' on his first.

In all cases the captain was **always** the pilot, and vice versa, no matter what his rank. Thus in the air, a sergeant could command a Flight Lieutenant or a Squadron Leader in the same crew. Often he was listed as taking up his CO, the Wing Commander, over whom, in the air, he had authority. Each was addressed by his nickname or his job, and the pilot as 'Skipper', surnames not being used for security reasons. The captain made the decisions and these were final, though he would take flight guidance from the navigator, airworthiness from the engineer, evasive action from the gunners, and target accuracy from the bomb aimer. Thus nicknames should be noted, they often suggest a clue to the searcher trying to decide between similar names.

SQUADRON NUMBERS   AIR 27 Series

NUMBERS 1 to 274 were inherited by the RAF from their RFC or RNAS originals. This indicates continuity from 1918 at the earliest. James Halley's book *Squadrons Of The RAF* and the three volumes on the open shelves at the PRO list each squadron, date of creation, places and dates where it served, aircraft used and their serial letters of identification. Included is also a potted history. Thus if the aircraft type and number are known, it should be possible to trace it to its squadron, and then, by date, to its crew. This is useful if photographs with machines are the only evidence.

Blocks of numbers after this indicate special roles, duties and nationalities. Roughly these are -

1	-	299	RAF	500 - 504	ex-AAF-Auxiliary Air Force or Special Reserve
300	-	309	Polish	510 - 539	RAF Special Duties
310	-	315	Czech	540 - 544	RAF PR-Photographic Reconnaissance
316	-	318	Polish	547 - 550	RAF
320	-	322	Dutch	567 - 598	RAF
326	-	329	Free French	600 - 616	ex-AAF
330	-	334	Norwegian	661 - 662	RAF-AOP (Air Observation Post)
335	-	336	Greek	663 -	Polish
340	-	347	Free French	664 - 666	RCAF AOP
348	-	350	Belgian	667 - 679	RAF
351	-	352	Yugoslav	680 - 684	RAF PR
400	-	445	RCAF	691 - 695	RAF
450	-	467	RAAF	900 - 947	RAF Balloon Squadrons
485	-	490	RNZAF	1435 -	RAF

Not every squadron number was used, as is indicated in Air 27, most of which is now on microfilm at the PRO, and several might need to be searched as a pilot could serve in more than one, some for a very short time.

Numbers 71, 121, 133 were initially the AMERICAN EAGLE SQUADRONS under RAF Command. They remained so until their American personnel were transferred in September 1942, to the USAAF. They were all volunteers who had usually come to the UK via Canada. (See later section).

As squadrons of all kinds were disbanded their records were passed to the Ministry of Defence and are held there until the **30 Year Rule** period has expired. Date of expiry for our purposes begins in 1972. They are now released yearly after that and filed with the rest. Do not expect to find everything about every squadron. Some records did not survive from the beginning, others have been weeded out, there are a few still retained for security reasons. Thus it is that not all records of the RAF are at Kew, though the majority required for genealogical and family history purposes are available.

THE AUXILIARY AIR FORCE at the outbreak of war in 1939 was able to mobilise twenty squadrons. Of these fourteen were in FIGHTER COMMAND, and the remaining six with COASTAL COMMAND and ARMY CO-OPERATION. In September 1939 they still retained their county or city titles - eg 605 was the County of Warwick Squadron - but all AAF personnel (who had been weekend or spare-time airmen of all ranks and jobs) were transferred to the RAF VOLUNTEER RESERVE. This is the significance of RAFVR after some names in the records books. They distinguished themselves from the VR proper by a small brass 'A' on their lapels, or in the case of airmen on the shoulder flash. The VR wore 'VR' in the same places. This of course caused a certain amount of rivalry, and in some cases friction, because an Auxiliary of any rank could not be posted away from his local base against his will. This was changed before the war was very old as it caused resentment.

The AAF was not re-established until June 1946, when many stayed on after demobilisation and increased their status in their spare time. In December 1947 the royal prefix was added by the assent of HM King George VI, and the AAF became the Royal Auxiliary Air Force and is still so today.

Many of the universities also had, and still have, a **University Air Squadron**, details of which can be established in the records of their parent university, and at the back of the AIR 27 Index.

RAF STATIONS

In 1939 there were about 170 airfields under the control of the RAF in the UK. Most of these were permanent and used by the Regulars or the Auxiliaries, so they were properly equipped and their housing was of brick to a formalised pattern. Later ones were hurriedly constructed and men often had to live in very uncomfortable conditions, sometimes under canvas. During the war and up to 1945 service construction departments and civil contractors between them built over 444 more airfields. Most of these have now been put to other uses. Some are used for civil flying or have become local airports - Manchester's Airport, Ringway, was No 1 Parachute Training School and 9 OTU at Crosby on Eden is the airport for Carlisle - but the small American base of the 14th Fighter Group of the USAAF at Atcham near Shrewsbury is reduced to cabbages and the once main runway is the road between two villages. In spite of being USAAF, it remained under RAF Command but was renamed Atcham Field. To find it and other US bases in the UK look first under its British name then in Air 40 and 45.

Once your man is found, it is worth filling in the background by looking at the places where he served. All have a very evocative atmosphere.

There were in total over 700 air bases on UK territory, including runway extensions, temporary parking bays, bases for flying boats such as at Pembroke Dock in Wales and Lough Erne in Northern Ireland. These included, after 1942 when the

USA had come into the war, those handed over to the USAAF. There were also many non-flying stations such as Maintenance Units, Training Schools for ground crew, storage depots, signals and medical units.

In the AIR class at Kew, look for these in AIR 27 for squadrons; AIR 28 by name; AIR 29 by description or function.

On the ground, station organisation was generally on three formal levels - Flying, Technical or Support, and Administration. Each was under the direction of a Wing Commander, who in turn was responsible to the Station Commander - usually a Group Captain or higher. Even if on the same base, these were called Wings, which in turn were divided into Squadrons, Flights and Sections. If not on the same base they were within the same Group and were near to each other. Each of the sub-divisions would have a nominal and frequently changing officer-commanding of established or war-rank.

Some of the high ranks among flying personnel seemed very young, the inference being there was no time to wait for peace-time procedure, and experience counted most. It was not unknown for Warrant Officers or NCOs in their early twenties like their senior officers, to hold the responsible positions.

It is important therefore not to confuse rank with age when hunting your quarry, nor to underestimate the responsibility of either. Of course the return to peace meant promotion was not quite as rapid as it had been, so be prepared for a difference after 1946 and more as the present day is approached.

NAME, RANK AND NUMBER - MANNING.

Three Squadrons usually made up a WING, each squadron having its own Commanding Officer - usually a Squadron Leader or a Wing Commander (the latter from 1940 on though the rank does not always describe the job). Each FLIGHT within a squadron (there were generally two, A and B, often one was for night the other for day) had a Flight Commander who was the senior and most experienced pilot, not necessarily an officer.

WINGS were under a Group Captain and GROUPS under an officer of Air rank, an Air Commodore or Air Vice Marshal. It follows that these were, of necessity, flexible rulings during the height of the war. After D Day when the air defence in Europe was called the 2nd TACTICAL AIR FORCE - written 2nd TAF - the three squadrons within a Wing were known collectively by their Wing number. Thus 124 Wing for part of that time consisted of 181, 182 and 247 Squadrons. As there was much exchange of pilots within a Wing at this period, start by looking under their Group HQ. 124 Wing was in 83 Group.

A, B and sometimes C Flights within a squadron were of equal importance. The existence of C depended on the size of the Wing and its function. Generally there was a support HQ Flight to accompany them for administration, usually staffed by older and non-flying men, also by WAAFs. These were similarly commanded.

Each machine had its own ground crew, which created a great bond of dependency between pilot, aircrew, and the mechanics and armourers who kept it flying, for which they all had deep affection.   These were a squadron's service echelon, generally identified by the number 6 prefixing the squadron number - but not always, so beware! Thus 6247 is 247's service unit. The ground staff consisted of all ranks up to Corporal, headed by a Sergeant in charge. A Flight Sergeant, denoted by a crown over his three chevrons, was over all and senior to an ordinary sergeant. 'Flight' indicates higher rank, not necessarily that he flew. Their superior officers were the engineering and maintenance officers of the unit, not the officers who flew the aircraft.

Towards the end of the war, this mutual dependence changed, when Service Echelons, commanded by the engineering officers, served the squadron as a whole, not individual aircraft.   Although the RAF is more democratic now and the bond between air and ground staff still strong, much of the personal loyalty to an individual aircraft and its crew has gone, to the regret of those who remember both systems. A story told by an ex- fighter pilot who helped with this guide illustrates this - coming back from a particularly gruelling dog-fight over London, he found the ground-crews of the machines usually in the parking bays either side his own with tears in their eyes because their pilots had 'bought it' and their aircraft 'gone for a Burton'.

SUBSTANTIVE, meaning confirmed, permanent and definite, was a peace time rank complicated by a war-time structure of promotion. It made provision for WAR SUBSTANTIVE, TEMPORARY AND ACTING ranks, both paid and unpaid. Unpaid does not mean the man received no pay, but that he was paid at the rate of his normal rank, and not that of his acting or temporary rank, which he could not claim until it was confirmed. Sometimes it never was.

During the **Battle Of Britain,** full substantive rank applied only to officers holding a regular commission. WAR SUBSTANTIVE rank was awarded to officers holding Temporary or Acting rank in place of certain people - eg the officer who took the CO's place while he was away sick, on leave or temporarily absent on duty elsewhere. TEMPORARY rank was for promotion by the AIR MINISTRY to fill vacancies in the wartime establishment.   ACTING rank was bestowed by

COMMANDS and GROUPS on officers performing the duties of certain higher ranks. Thus you will find T/F/Lt - Temporary Flight Lieutenant - and A/Sqn/Ldr/ - Acting Squadron Leader. Officers could hold higher rank than their genuine substantive rank for a considerable time before being promoted to a War Substantive rank - permanent for the duration.

All this needs expanding further but there is no room to do so here. Read, therefore, *The Royal Air Force Handbook 1939-45* by Chaz Bowyer, Ian Allan, Shepperton, Surrey.

Bear in mind, though, that peacetime formality was often bypassed in war as a matter of expediency, so that there could be a number of rapid, even if temporary, promotions at all levels. From 1941 on it was quite often found that Wings were commanded by very young Wing Commanders and Squadrons within them by equally young Squadron Leaders. At their ages before the war they would not have been considered to have sufficient seniority or sense of responsibility for a good leader. War was to disprove all that and, as they say, circumstances alter facts. After the war, however, promotion reverted to normal procedure and if Wing Commanders and Group Captains now look young to us it is only the 'young policeman' syndrome in action!

Even non-commissioned ranks could take command of a squadron or a flight if needs be and if the experience was there. Certainly in bomber crews non-commissioned pilots took command and took precedence. So do not be surprised at anything you find. There is always a reason.

The RAF, which had begun as a snobbish elitist organisation, in wartime progressed very quickly on the road to democracy and before long it was experience not rank which made a good operational leader. Junior NCOs were often promoted almost on the spot when necessary, which generally meant the squadron had suffered heavy losses. When the rank of a/sgt/pilot - acting sergeant pilot - occurs it means as in the commissioned ranks, not yet ratified. The derogatory title in WWI of 'temporary gentleman' does not apply to the RAF in WWII, but 'war substantive' does. It means he was not a career officer.

Likewise, RAF or RAFVR following the name means he was a REGULAR or a member of the pre-war all-rank VOLUNTEER RESERVE. RAFO means RESERVE OF AIR FORCE OFFICERS, those who had joined before the war or were time served but still on the Reserve.

AIRCREW

This is a generic term for everyone who flies, no matter what rank or in what capacity. A Captain generally chose his own crew wherever possible as soon as he and they became operational. Colloquially they were sometimes called 'the firm', and the cockpit was/is called 'the office'.

In 1940 it was decided that no airman below the rank of sergeant should take part in operations against the enemy. From that date all living aircrew were promoted immediately, past casualties were included. The effective date for the latter was that immediately prior to that of the casualty. Unfortunately little was done to implement this and the whole thing put aside and forgotten, consequently there are many below that rank in operations books and named on tombstones. Even so, all aircrew of whatever rank were and are volunteers. No-one was conscripted or directed into this particular branch of the service. Many, however, who aspired to be aircrew failed the stringent tests and were re-deployed.

All this must be taken into account if uncertain of the rank of the man sought. Some squadrons give service numbers, all give position in crew; bear in mind the pilot is the Captain even when higher ranks fly with him - but **none** give age or place of birth or parentage. These can sometimes be found in the **Commonwealth War Graves Commission indexes** (CWGC) - there is a full run at the Imperial War Museum (IWM) - or by letter from their office in Maidenhead. As well, many are in the records of escapers and evaders - WO208/3298 series (though an army file it gives RAF detail, because the Army was in charge of the interrogations).

Certain air force historians, such as those who researched and compiled the comprehensive book*The Battle Of Britain, Then And Now*, have tried wherever possible to rectify these forgotten promotions. Do not be surprised to find those of the lowest ranks of ACs 1 and 2 as part of a crew. Some may have been aircrew u/t - under training.

Of the aircrew killed in the Battle of Britain, six were only eighteen - George Brash, Maxwell Digby-Worsley, Laurie Rasmussen, Ronald Tucker, Daniel Wright, and the youngest AC2 Jacobson, rightfully a sergeant, who has no known grave. Several were reported missing or killed before they received their promotion and appear on the Commonwealth War Graves Commission tombstone with the lower rank and received its correspondingly lower rate of pay. Never, indeed, has so much been owed by so many to so few.

THE COMMONWEALTH WAR GRAVES COMMISSION puts up the standard issue tombstone wherever possible in the places where service people are buried - generally at home, near where they crashed, or in the churchyard nearest the unit's base. There are exceptions of course - those who were buried in family graves or like Billy Fiske, the first American to be killed in the Battle of Britain, at Boxgrove near Tangmere, West Sussex. There is a plaque to him in the crypt of St Paul's, but because America was not in the war in 1940, his family wanted him buried near to where he served and died, under a private stone.

If the fatality occurred in the UK, or death resulted from a crash, the name should be found in St Catherine's House in the usual way, or in the lists of war deaths there. Enquiries to the CWGC should be made to: 2 Marlow Road, Maidenhead, Berkshire SL6 7DX.

A register for every county in the UK is published and may be purchased. As well, there are registers for the other countries where the official tombstones have been erected. These lists are invaluable as they usually give as well as service number and rank, squadron or unit where known, age, next of kin and exactly where buried. It is a sad fact that there are more RAF graves near to training stations than elsewhere.

Those of no known grave are listed by year on the panels of the Runnymede Memorial near Windsor. Too many to list separately, but sections are available and individually priced from the above address. There is an annual remembrance ceremony for the next of kin, families and those connected.

ROLLS OF HONOUR

All squadrons kept their own Rolls of Honour and a great many more are to be found in various places and forms, the largest probably being that of the Runnymede Memorial. For instance I unexpectedly found a short one in the Guildhall at Much Wenlock, Shropshire. It was to an American bomber crew which crashed in the parish. There are full details to accompany it.

The grave of Sgt.Pilot Alan C.Kelly 40771 RNZAF, buried at St.Ilogan, near Portreath, North Cornwall, 247(F)(China British) Squadron, 10 Group.

This is the official headstone provided and cared for in such cemeteries by the Commonwealth War Graves Commission. Their index gives full details.

F/Lt John H Holloway took 14 years to complete his highly personalised roll containing over 2,200 names. He collected signatures from "The Few", adding to it even those of the dead from log books, driving licences, prayer books and the like, depositing the whole in the IWM. F/Lt Holloway was with 615 Squadron at RAF Kenley and retired in 1958.

There are some Rolls at the PRO in AIR 14/2091, and that of 115 Squadron is on the open shelves.

Bomber Command's own Roll is in Lincoln Cathedral, which is strategically placed more or less in the centre of the area from where the main bombing operations were initiated. The roll contains names from 1 and 5 Groups and may be inspected personally.

Westminster Abbey's Battle of Britain Chapel to the 63 squadrons which took part was dedicated on 10 July 1947. There are 448 names from Fighter command, 280 from Coastal, 14 in other RAF Commands and 34 of the Fleet Air Arm. 14 nations took part, and the 7 Americans who died are included.

The RAF's own church of St Clement Dane, in London, has a book of Remembrance. So do most of the cemeteries containing large numbers of RAF graves. The mammoth book *The Battle Of Britain, Then And Now* is a roll of honour in itself and a splendid piece of research.

Not all are listed in these records, there are bound to be omissions and errors. If your man is not there and you can prove he should be, his name can be added.

If you are interested in a particular squadron, it would be a labour of love to compile one for them.

LISTS of PRISONERS OF WAR in the AIR class at the PRO, Kew are in AIR 20/2336 - 1944 to 1945. These were notified via the RED CROSS in neutral Switzerland, to their opposite numbers in London, and sometimes these references appear also in squadron records. Most personal references however are still with their families. There are the interrogation reports of those who evaded capture in various countries, in WO 208 and in AIR 40/1897. The latter is by date of interrogation and return to this or other allied country. It includes all three services and is very useful as it gives date of birth, home address, pre-war occupation and air base from where started when landed in enemy territory. There is a full account of each man's experience, mentioning the fate of the rest of his crew, if known, as well as the people he met and who helped him.

The WAR OFFICE was responsible for the POWs of all services, so most coverage is found in WO 199/405-409. PRO Leaflet 111 *Prisoners of War and Displaced Persons 1939-1953: Documents in the PRO* gives full guidance.

EVADERS and ESCAPERS: in WO208 series. ESCAPING SOCIETY: in AIR 8/1428.

GROUND STAFF - on which every flier knew he was utterly dependent - have not been adequately researched and are very difficult to locate. Unless they did something to bring them to the attention of the command, they are rarely found in ops books. Some can be found in the Appendix volumes in the same AIR class indexes as their squadrons, others will be found in the daily routine orders of the base. In some cases where a complete unit was moved to another area, there may be a nominal roll. If found, this is invaluable as it gives name, rank, number and job, date when and how moved to the next station. This was made in order to account for who was to travel by air, by road and by train. A good example is given at the back of AIR 29/982 - when No 1 (C) OTU moved from Silloth to Thornaby on 8 March 1943. The OPERATIONAL TRAINING UNIT was moved by three air and three train parties so that every person is accounted for and listed, including those left behind on liaison.

Lists like these are not always recorded but are invaluable when they are. That they were made is incontestable. They were probably housed at Ruislip, the RAF Record Office at the time, of which the MOD's RAF Barnwood and Innsworth are the descendants. Unfortunately records there are not open to the public and may be approached only by letter.

For a full and complete account of RAF GROUND CREWS, read *From The Ground Up* by Fred Atkin, Airlife, 1983. The author joined the RAF aged 18 and served 22 years as an airframe fitter in most commands. Follow this up with *Behind The Hanger Doors.*

Originally the RAF in the UK was intended to consist mainly of bombers. The creation of FIGHTER COMMAND had to be hard fought for as any biography of Hugh, Lord Dowding describes. After the Invasion there is another area of command to add, by which a man's career may be followed through France, Belgium and Holland into Germany. This was -

THE ALLIED EXPEDITIONARY AIR FORCE which came into being on 13 November 1943. Under the command of Air Chief Marshal Sir Trafford Leigh-Mallory it had three main components, for which there had been preparations on a secret but grand scale for the whole of the previous year - the US 9th AIR FORCE which was already in existence - FIGHTER COMMAND which as such was dissolved becoming the 2nd TACTICAL AIR FORCE (2nd TAF) - and the AIR DEFENCE OF GREAT BRITAIN (ADGB).

Of these, 83 Group was originally called Z or Composite Group and was fed by the lessons learnt in the 'SPARTAN' exercise. Thus, when these three names are found in AIR 27's squadron records, they refer to the same thing - preparation for D Day and the forming of the 2nd TAF (AIR 37). This and other GROUPS involved should be looked for under AIR 25 and cross-referenced in AIR 37. Each should then be subdivided again into WINGS and back again via individual SQUADRONS in AIR 27.

83 GROUP'S BATTLE ORDER, for example, is in AIR 37/401 but is changed almost daily. Useful if you know your man's base only by its code number, as squadrons used both name and number eg:- B6 was St Croix-sur-Mer in June 1944 - B58 was Melsbroek, Brussels, in which city was 83 Group's HQ - B78 was Eindhoven - B156 Luneberg - B58 Lubeck and so on.

The construction of a GROUP should be familiar to genealogists as its 'family tree' is generally illustrated. This will give you everything which operated within that Group. All that then needs to be done is to cross reference these by name in the relevant AIR class index files, or by number if a squadron. Isolate these by year and more than likely your man, if aircrew, is listed there.

If other than aircrew, the whole of the GROUP's records must be combed for clues, and it isn't easy. Occasionally there are NOMINAL ROLLS and records of promotions, awards and misdemeanours. Do not expect to find other than a brief mention of courts martial, these are closed.

Gradually, from the end of this long period in Europe, there begin to be records of discharges and releases, and from 1945-46 they become quite frequent. These you will need if you want to mark the end of a service career and the beginning of a new civilian life but it should not be forgotten that many signed on for a longer period and were not time- expired until much later. Do not confuse time-expired with tour-expired; the latter applies mainly to aircrews who, for safety's sake, were permitted only a given number of operational sorties, though these were often exceeded. Tour-expired does not mean left the service, only a temporary change of direction.

AIRCRAFTMEN WHO KEPT THE PILOTS FLYING

247(F)(China British)Squadron ground staff at High Ercall, Shropshire.
Published by kind permission of George Woodruff.

April 1943, Site 6.
Back row - LACs Kirby, Lewis, Ramsden, Cpl.Cowley, LAC Judge.
Front row - Aircraftman Speakman and Mooney, Sgt.Collins.

OVERSEAS SERVICE

Whilst many squadrons remained on home defence for the entire duration of the war, there were several, originally in the UK, which were later posted abroad. Almost all the home defence squadrons did some time in France until the fall of that country in 1940. Those sent abroad can be ascertained and the homework done on dates and aircraft before beginning the search. James Halley's *Squadrons Of The RAF*, Air Britain, updated frequently, (a copy of which is on the open shelves at Kew) lists them all by number, giving the places where they were stationed. The operations books are then looked for in the usual way in AIR 27.

If only the overseas base name is known, then look in AIR 28 and 29.

OVERSEAS COMMANDS in general are in AIR 32. (PRO Leaflet 16 *Operational Records Of The RAF*, gives further guidance). There are different Group numbers for these. Though rumours abounded, a squadron was not always told until a few days before the move overseas when leave was suddenly cancelled and those away recalled. Sometimes this security was broken and the whole operation cancelled because of a leak. Often they did not know where they were going until, on board the troopship, tropical kit or similar was issued. There were times when the contrary kit was given out to fool the enemy should a leak still occur. Again, do not be surprised.

Be careful not to confuse the number of a home-based squadron with a similar one allocated to the air forces of the Commonwealth. 10 Squadron, for example, if home based, had that number only, whereas 10 RCAF indicated a Canadian Squadron. RCAF Squadrons in the UK were usually numbered in the 400 series. Some squadrons like Number 60 never served at home at all. All and any of them could, of course, serve in any theatre of war.

The Appendix details apply to these overseas stations in the same way as to any other, but again, may not have survived. Take into account, too, the conditions abroad - for example, during the evacuation of Greece and Crete, it was difficult enough to get the men out and not all did. Paper work therefore was secondary, and for many squadrons involved there are no records at all. Therefore even fewer documents recording overseas service may have survived than were safely rescued at home.

For the South African Air Force, generally speaking, records are only on microfilm, though there are many mentions of SAAF personnel serving in RAF squadrons. There is a leaflet explaining the microfilm records.

WAAF - WOMEN'S AUXILIARY AIR FORCE

THE WAAFs originated in the Women's Auxiliary Army Corps formed in 1917, accepting women for non-combative duties behind the lines. Later that year the WOMEN'S ROYAL NAVAL SERVICE was formed. There was also the WOMEN'S LEGION which was a corps providing drivers of cars and other vehicles for the military. When the RFC and the RNAS were separately and independently formed, it was decided that a WOMEN'S AIR FORCE CORPS should also be formed to support the RFC with clerical and sick quarter nursing services. It was so called until 1920 and the WOMEN'S ROYAL AIR FORCE when it was disbanded. Over 32,000 had served in its ranks.

In 1938 the AUXILIARY TERRITORIAL SERVICE - ATS - was formed. Within it were included companies which had a particular reference to the RAF, and though not designated as such, the ATS was its support and clerical unit as its predecessor had been for the RFC. In that same year the first of these women's RAF Companies was affiliated to No 601 Auxiliary Air Force Squadron at Kidbrooke. From there its essential support was obvious and its possibilities widened.

Early in 1939 the AIR COUNCIL agreed that it would be both suitable and more appropriate if a separate women's service were to be formed and called the WOMEN'S AUXILIARY AIR FORCE. So the WAAFs were born in June 1939 with Miss Jane Trefusis as their first WAAF Director. She was ranked as a Senior Controller, wearing the sleeve rank badges of an Air Commodore.

The first WAAF RECRUITMENT DEPOT was at West Drayton and remained there until Sept 1940. The WAAFs were then moved to Harrogate, as No 1 Depot.

No 2 Depot opened at Innsworth as the CENTRAL TRAINING AND RECEPTION DEPOT for Southern England.

No 3 Depot opened in October 1941 at Morecambe, but closed in 1943. Wilmslow took over for the North until August 1943 and from then on received all new recruits for WAAF training.

Not entirely separate from its parent the RAF, as was the ATS from the Army, it was part of the main framework and support of the air force. Yet it served under an entirely different discipline, so that the powers of command of WAAF officers and NCOs over **any RAF** male of **any** rank were severely restricted. Not so today when a FLIGHT LIEUTENANT is what it says, the sex is immaterial to the authority!

In fact it was not compulsory for other ranks in the RAF to salute WAAF officers, and it was dependent upon their good manners, not enforceable on station and in uniform, as between men. Attitude and acceptance played a large part. All RAF officers and NCOs had almost full power over airwomen in work and discipline situations, regardless of the wishes of their own female officers.

Unlike RAF personnel, between 1939-41 WAAFs could not be charged with desertion, or with being absent without leave, nor could they be severely disciplined within their own unit. Misdemeanours could only be dealt with by court martial at which WAAF officers could not sit as members of the panel. Indeed a WAAF officer, within the meaning of the Air Force Act, was not an officer at all. An extraordinary situation which makes searching for women in the RAF - in which they played a great part, later fully acknowledged, and on whom so much depended - a very difficult task.

Many RAF Station Commanders as well as other officers refused to take WAAFs seriously as service personnel, regarding them as decoration only, until they had no other choice. Though subject to the same rules of postings that seemed to move their male counterparts about the country in apparently meaningless journeys, WAAFs had certain privileges which men were not offered. A WAAF married to an RAF serviceman could ask to be posted to his station with him when he was posted out. Sisters could ask to serve together. This latter was only granted to brothers if they were twins, unless strings could be pulled (as they undoubtedly were). This makes the chances of finding WAAFs in the records problematic.

Although taking the place of men to release them for 'more important work', women were never accepted as aircrew in spite of there being many competent women pilots in the ATA (AIR TRANSPORT AUXILIARY) and in FERRY COMMAND.

They did, however, assume the rank of those they released in clerical duties, serving as radio operators, mechanics, fitters, drivers, kitchen staff, batmen, as well as bombing-up and operating radar. Indeed many women fitters and mechanics were allowed to fly with their pilots as passengers but only to check their work. Many, even so, managed a 'jolly' now and then.

For further information see Chaz Bowyer's *Royal Air Force Handbook;* F J Adkin's *From The Ground Up;* the *AHB narratives AIR 2/4026 and AIR 6/39; Wings On Her Shoulder* by Katherine Bentley Beaumont and *Partners In Blue* by the same author and *Women In Air Force Blue* by Sqn Ldr Beryl Escott, Patrick Stephens, 1989. See Bibliography. See also list sent to the Fawcett Library (Womens' History)

Here is where a geographical knowledge of the area is useful as the WAAF base did not always carry the same name as that of its RAF parent, and local history may have to be consulted in order to find which stately home was requisitioned, if the women were not on a hutted site. One example is Attingham Hall near Atcham, Shropshire - home to the WAAFs of RAF Atcham. It is said in the local records that little damage was found when the house was at last de-requisitioned, which is more than can be said of most houses in similar situations. RAF aircrews were given to boisterous games, encouraged by their CO, as they released tension.

This house is detailed in the AIR records but the full story can only be found in the **County Record Office,** at Shrewsbury. Equally, until their Mess was properly established at the same base, the Mytton and Mermaid Hotel was used by the officers. At Exeter, the George and Dragon public house was the sergeant's mess for 247(F)Squadron, also findable in the local **Record Office.**

What there is to be found on WAAFs is scattered through the operations books related to their station, the daily routine orders, sick quarters records and under WOMEN'S AUXILIARY AIR FORCE in the AIR index. Since there was not the same structure of training as there was for aircrew, this is bound to be difficult and patience is required. Look in the index AIR 2 for further detail.

There is, however, one very useful document in AIR 24/1640 to 46, covering 1940 to 1943 only. There was an instruction at this time for WAAF units to submit a narrative history of the formation of their particular unit and its duties. How many of these were compiled in full is not known, but those who complied did so in an informal manner written by the women themselves, refreshingly different from the strict adherence to form which characterised the operational record books of the men. Useful but not comprehensive, each batch has a list of stations covered. These, therefore, should be consulted and compared with the records of their main RAF parent station. These unofficial logs **may** contain the names you are looking for. That, for instance, of A.M.E.S. Drone Hill at Berwick includes signatures which are useful for comparison. (See also NOMINAL ROLLS).

At the outbreak of war there were 48 WAAF companies containing 230 officers and 7460 airwomen. At their peak strength the WAAFs numbered 181,909 women in 1943 and by the end of the war over 80 different trades were listed including 21 concerned with direct maintenance and servicing of aircraft. Apart from the secret CODE AND CYPHER 'Y' Service, for which you will find many posted-in, the WAAF played an essential part in the radar chain and other forms of Intelligence. See *The Enemy Is Listening* by Aileen Clayton, Hutchinson, 1980, and *Evidence In Camera* by Constance Babbington-Smith, David and Charles, 1957, who discovered the bases at Peenemunde from photographs in May 1942. The V1 rockets or pilotless planes, so devastating to London, were launched from here.

Royal Flying Corps
Cap Badge

Pilot
R.F.C.

Shoulder Title

Shoulder Title

Flight Sergeant
R.F.C.

UNIFORMS

IDENTIFYING THE SUBJECT FROM HIS/HER UNIFORM

This is not as easy with RAF uniforms as it may be with photographs of soldiers of different regiments and dates. For one thing, regimental buttons have different patterns and are often set on the tunic in different alignments. Army cap badges vary in shape according to the regiment or corps. There have been few major changes in RAF uniforms since the stand collar and breeches of the RFC gave way to the less stiff tunic and the more comfortable collar, tie and trousers. There was little difference in the patterns of uniform of officers and other ranks, except in the quality of the cloth, and during the war everyone wore the same kind of battle- blouse, except in the mess and on formal occasions. Overalls are now worn on the base and there is little difference in anyone's clothing.

The "erk" or aircraftman/woman wore a tunic with a belt of the same fabric: this has now gone and the tunic fits better and is more flattering. The "fore and aft" or side cap was a matter of personal choice, and is seldom now worn by officers. The cap badge - a circular wreath for other ranks, and an eagle and crown for officers, - is the only obvious difference if rank markings cannot be discerned. The flat peaked cap has come back into fashion. In 1939, the officer's cap had, and still has, a matching peak, with a wide band of black braid bearing a wreath and the eagle and crown. If of Group Captain status or higher, there are gold leaves on the peak. The peak of an other rank's cap was shiny black. WAAFs' uniforms were much the same with the option of trousers to wear on station and skirts off duty. Rank markings were on the sleeves or shoulders for everybody. Now many of these are replaced by patches, except in the case of officers' best blue and formal dress. Buttons are standard throughout the service irrespective of status or trade.

PHOTOGRAPHS themselves do not help a great deal unless there is an aircraft in the background. This at least establishes the kind and function of the squadron we are looking at. Sometimes an aircraft's markings are of help, and certainly its number and letters can identify a squadron. The number is its individual registration and, like a car's, remains with it no matter who is the owner. The letters indicate the squadron to which it belongs and can be changed. Camouflage or colouring may vary with squadron duty. For example, fighter type aircraft on reconnaissance photography, usually Spitfires, were painted a light duck egg blue to blend with the sky in which, because they were unarmed, they flew very high. [See AIRCRAFT and illustrations of various markings in the book *Hawker Hurricane* by Francis K. Mason, 1987, Aston Publications. This book contains references to many other more general identifying features such as squadron commanders' pennants, etc.

Among fliers there were a great many personal idiosyncrasies, but button pattern and colour of uniform, being standard, betray nothing. Even so RANK BADGES on the sleeve, whether for commissioned rank or not, are helpful. In battledress or tunic-less shirt, officers wore theirs on the shoulder strap. The double chevron of the Corporal and the triple chevron of the Sergeant are easily recognised. A light blue wreath on black near the cuff indicates a Warrant Officer. All ranks below NCO had a shoulder flash of an eagle in light blue on black, whilst the LAC - leading aircraftman/woman - also had a light blue embroidered propeller on the upper sleeve. It should be noted that the uniform cloth used by the Australian Air Force was a very dark blue.

Pilot Officer is the lowest commissioned rank, but the name does not imply that the officer is a pilot (brevet over the left pocket indicates a flier). The badge of rank is a thin light blue stripe (often called half stripe or ring) around the cuff. The next rank is Flying Officer with a slightly wider stripe, followed by Flight Lieutenant with two of these wider stripes. A Squadron Leader has two and half stripes, a Wing Commander, three and a Group Captain, four. The nomenclature is somewhat confusing as a Flight Lieutenant is not always responsible for a flight and a Squadron Leader does not necessarily lead or command a squadron. These are ranks created by promotion, they are not necessarily a job description. This applies to all ranks as an aircraftman/woman may never see an aircraft for example if they are serving on a non-flying station. Nowadays virtually all aircrew are commissioned, although there are still exceptions. During training aircrew, commissioned or not, wore a white flash in the front of their forage caps or a white band around their flat peaked caps.

A PILOT wears his double winged brevet either side of the RAF wreath and crown, together with any medal ribbons, all above the left breast pocket. A Polish pilot wore a metal eagle suspended by a chain from under these wings. Pathfinder pilots and aircrew, abbreviated to PFF, wore the RAF eagle (as on an officer's side cap) on the pocket under the wings. Australian aircrew carried a miniature of the same on the sleeve above their rank rings.

An OBSERVER's "O" had a single wing; the NAVIGATOR who replaced him in 1942 had an N in a wreath, in lieu of the "O". The AIR GUNNER also had a single wing with AG in the wreath. FLIGHT ENGINEER had an "E" and WIRELESS OPERATOR, "WOP" although the latter's job was often amalgamated with that of Air Gunner. With the development of air electronics many of these designations, with the exception of pilot and navigator, have changed and others have been added. It is not advisable to take modern markings and brevet as a guide.

For aircrew liable to come down in enemy territory, special buttons were issued during WWII but although sometimes of black composition, appear to be the normal standard pattern. Examples can be seen at the **RAF Museum, Hendon**. They often contained a compass or a radio. Aircrew were also issued with a small whistle, used for locating each other if lost on the ground or in the sea, and this can be seen in some photographs.

Fighter pilots often wore the top tunic button undone but were discouraged from doing so when flying, and to do so before proving oneself was "shooting a line". The spotted silk foulard is part of the fighter pilot's unofficial uniform as is the white polo-necked sweater and long white silk scarf. These were not just a Biggles affectation; real silk has warmth not in other materials, and warmth at great heights and high speeds was necessary. Modern aircrew have heated suits and cockpits. In emergency situations garments which were white, showed up at night and over a long distance in much the same way as the yellow dinghies.

The MEDICAL OFFICER has metal caducees on his lapel; the CHAPLAIN, a cross. Both, unless the circumstances are exceptional, are of ground rank although they often have flying experience.

Many airman and airwomen of all ranks today wear sweaters, with indications of rank on the shoulder reinforcement. This was not customary or official in WWII. There are many more clues to be found in books on modern uniforms. INSIGNIA and patches are now collectors' items and can be bought at many air-shows and museums, those of the RFC and WWI being the rarest and most valuable. All aircrew wore leather flying jackets and boots lined and edged with sheepskin, the precursors of both types of clothing worn today. Before 1942, when the U.S.A. came into the War, one-piece Irvin suits, with multi-pockets and zippers, were more usual. Many of

OFFICER'S
FORAGE
CAP
BADGE
R.A.F.

ROYAL AIR FORCE
(Cap Badge)

ROYAL AIR FORCE
(Cap Badge)

CAP BADGE worn by officers below air rank consists of the Crown, Eagle and Wreath. Officers of the W.A.A.F. and the Princess Mary's R.A.F. Nursing Service wear a similar badge. Rankers and members of the Women's Auxiliary Air Force wear the monogram R.A.F., surrounded by a wreath and surmounted by a crown.

ROYAL AIR FORCE
MEDICAL SERVICE
COLLAR BADGE

ROYAL AIR FORCE
(Pilot's Wings)

OBSERVER

GUNNER

EMBLEMS OF AIR FORCE RANKS

MARSHAL OF THE
ROYAL AIR FORCE

AIR CHIEF MARSHAL

AIR MARSHAL

AIR VICE-MARSHAL

AIR COMMODORE

GROUP CAPTAIN

WING COMMANDER

SQUADRON LEADER

FLIGHT-LIEUTENANT

FLYING OFFICER

PILOT OFFICER

these were heated as most aircraft of that period were not. In addition aircrew wore the inflatable jacket known, for obvious reasons, as the **Mae West**. This was bright yellow and kept its wearer afloat if he ditched in the sea.

RIBBONS were not always worn, although medal-holders were supposed to wear them on their uniform. The most easily identified ribbon, with purple and white diagonal stripes, relates to the DFC awarded to commissioned ranks. Other ranks were awarded the DFM having a similarly coloured ribbon but with narrower stripes. A small gilt rose on the ribbon refers to a BAR or second award of the decoration. Many other decorations can be found, graphically illustrated, in *Ribbons And Medals* by the author of adventure fiction whose pseudonym was Taffrail - H. Tapprell Dorling. Most recipients of awards are mentioned in Squadron records, but they themselves were, and are, modest and seldom mention them or tell the reason why they were given. Questioned, one answer was "Given out with the Christmas stocking". Don't be tempted to believe this; a man who had any of these awards was courageous.

Sergeant in the Medical Branch of the RAF - chevrons (stripes) on both arms, caducees on lapels, ground staff patch on each shoulder, campaign medal ribbons over left pocket. Brass buttons with RAF crown and eagle. Note flat hat with brass badge and shiny black peak with strap. Kidbrooke 1952.
By kind permission of Harry Leathers, member of the Guild of One-Name Studies, formerly 625323 Sgt Leathers H.A., enlisted 1938, retired 1968.

Details of such awards and others, if the date is known, can be found in the LONDON GAZETTE; ZJ1/- is the class reference followed by the piece number by date. AWARDS AND DECORATIONS are dealt with more fully in Part II. See also AIR 30.

Two NCO pilots showing informal (left) and formal (right) uniforms: 1940- 41.

Greaves on the left, wearing battle dress and flying boots, with polo neck pullover and forage or side cap.

Forman on the right, wearing tunic and collar and tie. Leather gloves for pilots were necessary, with silk gloves inside for warmth, as there was no heating in the cockpit. Both were sergeants, when Forman became a Flight Sergeant there was a brass crown above the 'V' of his stripes.

MODERN RANK DESIGNATION

Warrant Officer

Master Aircrew

Flight Sergeant

Sergeant Aircrew

Corporal

Flight Sergeant Aircrew

Chief Technician

Sergeant

Junior Technician

**Senior Aircraftman and
Senior Aircraftwoman**

**Leading Aircraftman and
Leading Aircraftwoman**

Pub. 526.   Produced on behalf of the Royal Air Force by Rapier Arts Limited.

Pilot on left is Canadian: note shoulder flash, and rank of Sqn Ldr at cuff of tunic. Colloquially two-and-a-half stripes.   He was aged 23 and the CO. He is wearing an uninflated Mae West; in his left hand are his goggles and the necessary plugs for his helmet. Note the scarf replacing collar and tie.

Pilot on right is Free French: sometimes described as Fighting French. He too has a shoulder flash, but it is hidden by the parachute he is carrying. He is wearing a battle blouse, unlike the other pilot. Although in a British squadron (247)(F) his aircraft carries the Free French Cross of Lorraine.

PART II

ROYAL AIR FORCE RECORDS AT THE PUBLIC RECORD OFFICE, KEW

There are many other places besides the Public Record Office where air records may be found, some of which have been mentioned already, but the PRO Kew is the starting point after the homework, and the source to which the researcher will return again and again. It is also the only place accessible to the public, where the original records made in situ, and often in the heat of the battle, are available.

Many of these are now too fragile for continued use and are on microfilm. At present a great deal of AIR 27, the squadron records, are on film and cannot be looked at in the original. Disappointing but necessary. At the time of writing, AIR 28 and 29, the original station or unit records, are still available. Do take care of them, please, as some of these are very fragile. **Do not** be tempted to alter or correct anything, no matter how wrongly your name is spelled or how mistaken you think the facts. There is a self-service photocopier in the micro room.

Initially to use the PRO you will need identification to gain a reader's ticket and number. Then, go up to the first floor reception where, in a help-yourself pigeon hole, are leaflets to guide you to the records. At least two of these are useful for the first-time RAF researcher - No.13 *Air Records as Sources for Biography and History* and No.16 *Operational Records of the Royal Air Force* especially. Others tell you how to use the PRO generally. There is a noticeboard to which requests and queries may be pinned. First go to the distribution desk and ask for a bleeper: this will give you a seat number.

The AIR class records will be the ones you use most. There are three sets of indexes - to the left outside the main reference room door in green binders, or either side of the door inside, in red binders. If stuck, ask at the main desk. Remember pencils only are allowed and silence is observed in the main reading room. Take plenty of paper.

The AIR class covers all aspects of aviation history, including WWI and the RFC but it is AIR 27, 28 and 29 which are the most useful for starters. Method of ordering from these is explained at the computer terminals, activated by taking the piece number on the left. Ignore the right hand column.

If it is OPERATIONAL SQUADRONS and their crews which are needed, then AIR 27 is where to begin. Look for the squadron number and note the piece number on the left by year. Numbers on the right can be ignored. Go to the computer terminal, put in your reader's ticket number, the desk number at which you are sitting, followed by the class and its number, then finally the piece number. When your order comes up from the stock, your bleeper will call you from any place in the building.

AIR 27 will tell you the squadron number, where it was stationed, who the CO was - not necessarily the Station Commander, he will be in the station's records. It lists, on Form 540, the daily record of work projected followed by a monthly summary of what was actually done and a lot more besides. It will tell you the crews of a BOMBER SQUADRON, their ranks and jobs, and their captain, plus their target for that day or night, bomb load carried, and what happened, or the full complement of a FIGHTER SQUADRON'S pilots, the object of their exercise and the result. In both cases it will tell you the order of take-off (by letter), the type and mark of each aircraft and its individual number. Thus you can trace the life history of an aircraft as well as its crew. From time to time it will tell you of promotions and decorations, postings-in and out, and often where from and where to, so you can follow your man

THE PUBLIC RECORD OFFICE, KEW

backwards or forwards. On the right there is a reference to an Appendix number, which you will find listed also by year in AIR 27. These have not always survived, but worth looking for. There is also a weather report.

Each month is recorded separately. In the summary you **may** find personal information, such as marriages and births of children, but it was not compulsory to record them. Regard them as a bonus and, if found, cross check at St Catherine's House, London - the General Register Office. There are **no** personal details - you will not find how much your man was paid, who his parents were, his wife's name, nor will you know how tall he was, or where there was a birthmark. You will not even learn when he joined or what his job was before doing so. Since it is likely he is still alive, or his next of kin are, these details are not disclosed.

The summary depended on the personality of the man who wrote it. Some regarded it only as a necessary chore. There was no strict rule to be adhered to, and in spite of admonishment from on high and reminders from Civil Service authority, some are very carelessly kept. So it is up to the searcher to find other records to fill in the gaps. Do not be too critical, however. Remember under what stress some must have been compiled.

The squadron's or unit's history from its formation and inaugural date, giving the names of the initial and administration staff and their postings-in, is usually in the first of these books. Some date from 1918. The detail varies according to the interest of the compiling officer, usually but not always the adjutant. The whole is generally signed by the CO or his deputy, so again, you can make cross reference with your man's LOG BOOK, if you or he still has it. If not, there are a few at the PRO, and some at the RAF Museum. See separate section.

Most officers can be located via the AIR FORCE LIST, on the open shelves. This gives squadron allocation only in the early years, but does give his number and seniority, thus you can make a guess at when he was commissioned. Be careful though, when commissioned from the ranks as most were unless regulars, the service number changes. An airman or NCO and an officer may be one and the same man but the number, though the same for the first two, will change on commissioning. (see separate section.)

OTHER AIR CLASS NUMBERS

Although AIR 27, 28 and 29 are the main reference indexes leading to the rest, there are many others to which the search may be directed. Within each one the separate piece numbers - on the left - may contain the clue needed to go further. These are -
COMMANDS AIR 24   GROUPS   AIR 25   WINGS   AIR 26
SQUADRONS AIR 27 UK,   ALLIED and COMMONWEALTH
STATIONS   AIR 28 UK, and OVERSEAS   MISCELLANEOUS UNITS AIR 29
2nd TAF   AIR 37 and others (Tactical Air Force, in Europe, after 1943 -
                 though still under squadron number in Air 27)
After D Day Fighter Command was divided into AIR DEFENCE OF GREAT BRITAIN (ADGB) and 2nd TAF.
BOOKS CONTAINING OVER-ALL INFORMATION, but with special reference to, the PRO at KEW. Some may be in the PRO's own library.
The RAF in general: *Portal Of Hungerford* by Denis Richards, Heinemann, 1977, gives the PRO AIR and other class references to everything consulted: also the the reference numbers to material at the AIR HISTORICAL BRANCH of the MoD, and at the RAF Museum, Hendon.

FIGHTER COMMAND: *Fighter, the story of the Battle Of Britain* by Len Deighton, Panther, 1979, has a chronological list of dates and events, RAF Squadrons and Luftwaffe involved, as well as maps and diagrams and a full plan of the groups and stations taking part. Adolf Galland, Germany's great fighter pilot, gives an account from the other point of view in *The First And The Last*, Collins/Fontana, 1970. The most detailed book however, with a full list of pilots' names, is *The Narrow Margin* by Derek Wood and Derek Dempster, Arrow/Hutchinson, 1961. This has a daily log but also a much wider coverage of Groups and their Commanding Officers, RAF Stations and the Squadrons based at each.

BOMBER COMMAND: *The Bomber Command War Diaries*, by Martin Middlebrook and Chris Everitt, Viking, 1985, subtitled "An Operational Reference Book", is indeed that. Listed are all the Squadrons by number, their Group and Station, together with the PRO AIR CLASS REFERENCE NUMBERS and many other sources of valuable reference material.

Armed with these references, it is worth while compiling your own, if your project is a piece of serious research. A great deal of value is located at the PRO and discovered by accident, for the indexes cannot possibly include all that is within their general titles. CROSS REFERENCE is one of the most important tools of research such as this, for things like the weather, pilots' and crews' health and morale, played as great a part as anything else in determining whether or not a squadron was successful in its objective. Many other records relating to such subjects are uncovered by a browse through the non-obvious class and piece numbers.

FOLLOWING HIS CAREER

In AIR 29, MISCELLANEOUS UNITS, it is possible to find units difficult to locate elsewhere. All are described - ITW (Initial Training Wings), Medical Schools, RAF Regiment (identified by squadron numbers), Maintenance Units, Technical and Engineering Branches, etc.

All these contain squadrons which served under British command, with the exception of some South African Air Force (SAAF) Squadrons whose Ops Books are on microfilm in AIR 54, which contains details of various operational units serving in Africa, the Middle East and the Mediterranean.

COMMANDS can be broken down still further. From 1936 on these show the planning and conduct of the above operations, they are the records and daily routine of the various headquarters. It is advisable to look in these if you are not sure where a particular unit served or what it did:-

BOMBER COMMAND	AIR 14	COASTAL COMMAND	AIR 15
FIGHTER COMMAND	AIR 16	BALLOON COMMAND	AIR 13
MAINTENANCE COMMAND	AIR 17	(relates to the MUs)	
OVERSEAS COMMAND	AIR 23	ARMY CO-OPERATION	AIR 39
FERRY & TRANSPORT COMMAND	AIR 38	(See also Air Transport Auxiliary, ATA in the AVIA class)	
TRAINING COMMAND	AIR 32		

These are not easy records to use, and stress is again laid on the need for homework and background reading, if there is to be any success. At first they will all be difficult to understand, especially if you were not in the RAF yourself, but gradually the unfamiliar terms become clear and the method of procedure easier to follow.

With 2nd Tactical Air Force Records, the method is similar. But although there is a wealth of material grouped under this title, it is still necessary to look for squadrons by number in spite of their being grouped into Wings and Airfields. 2nd TAF served in Europe after D Day. AIR 16/117, AIR 20/1593-4, AIR 24/1496 and AIR 37 etc. **give details**. This done, further cross-referencing, such as the ORDER OF BATTLE, may be made in GROUP Records - AIR 25. Remembering the Divisions is essential - Groups were divided into Wings and these into Squadrons. Some Squadrons at this period operated from Southern England, and their airfields are often given the same number as the Wing. Once into Europe, however, these airfields, for security reasons, had B numbers. These will all be found in Group Records. For example, 83 Group had within it 122 Wing HQ which was at Grimberghen, numbered B60. Within that Wing were 19, 65 and 122 Squadrons all of which flew Mustang 111s. Also in 83 Group was 126 RCAF Wing at Le Culot, B68, with 401, 411, 412, and 442 RCAF Squadrons all with Spitfire IX LFs. All this, and more, is in AIR 25, in which casualties also are listed. Casualties in 2nd TAF are also in AIR 37.

POSITION IN BOMBER CREW, as listed in Ops Books in AIR 27
1   Pilot/Captain

2   Navigator - nav - earlier years could be Observer

3   Air Bomber - a/bmr or bomb aimer

4   Wireless Operator - w/op, and/or Air Gunner - a/g;if combined wop/ag

5   Flight Engineer - f/eng

6   Air Gunner or Mid Upper Gunner - a/g or m.u.g

7   Air Gunner - Rear, r/g or "Tail-end-Charlie"

This may vary according to the number in the crew and the size of the aircraft, but is substantially correct. The pilot, of whatever rank, always heads the list.

AIR 27 gives postings-in and out and from this his service history may be followed. This recording pattern is not strictly adhered to although it is general. Aircraft numbers, type and order of take-off, are located in this series.

OTUs also kept Ops Books (ORBs) though not in quite the same way since OPERATIONAL TRAINING UNITS were not often used against the enemy if it could be avoided. Name of the place, if not the number, is essential in locating these in AIR 28 and 29. They were sometimes moved about from vulnerable areas to others less so. It is in this movement you may find NOMINAL ROLLS. Read carefully, the place and number was often changed for security reasons. These were, after all, the seed corn of the RAF's strength with which the operational squadrons were fed. It was the final stage of training for aircrew. They were not supposed to go on, or be used on, bombing missions, but were so on many occasions when the front line squadrons were at low ebb. Their instructors were fully trained, long- experienced officers and

NCOs, often sent there for a "rest". Many of these instructors preferred the front line, regarding it as less hazardous. Pupils are described as u/t - under training. Here too you will find many mentions of ATC squadrons - AIR TRAINING CORPS boys - being taken up for experience. Some you will find among the casualties. Do not confuse with ATC - Air Traffic Control.

An all-OTU crew was never used against the enemy, but some may have served as such under experienced captains. Thus was this seed corn often wasted out of sheer necessity.

If your man was an instructor he is likely to be found here.

TRAINING

This is a wide subject which may come under a variety of headings. Look first into AIR 29 under the many kinds of training units - INITIAL TRAINING WING (ITW), ELEMENTARY FLYING TRAINING SCHOOLS (EFTS), etc on to OPERATIONAL TRAINING UNITS, the OTUs already discussed. There are many others to be found in the same index - the procedure for calling them up on the computer is the same.

There were others in different parts of the Commonwealth, which were opened up when the United Kingdom became threatened by invasion and the RAF was particularly vulnerable. Find these, for instance, in RAF OTUs in the USA in AIR 45/11, 16 and 17, and 111 OTU in the Bahamas in AIR 45/18, 19 and 20. The Empire Training Scheme in Canada will be found in AIR 46, and by name in AIR 28, or such as 39 SFTS in Saskatchewan, in AIR 29/585. South African Air Force Ops Books are on micro AIR 54.

Look for other countries which took part - such as Australia and Rhodesia (not Zimbabwe then) under that country's name and the OTU's number, and again cross reference by name in AIR 28. This may require more patience and more homework, remembering that OTUs do not always have photographs nor do they always give the names of the course pupils. Some, such as the *Arnold Scheme,* produced a booklet which listed the names and the original hometowns of each man. If found among his souvenirs this is treasure, if not, his year of intake must be known.

The *Arnold Scheme* in America, named from the US General who instigated the plan, may be found in AIR 2/8095 and under the individual names of the parent air force bases. The *Towers Scheme* was similar. There is an *Arnold Register* which lists and indexes those who were trained as part of these schemes - 51, Henley Road, Leicester, LE3 9RD. An sae or 3 IRCs (for overseas enquiries) will bring advice.

The chapter on Training in Chaz Bowyer's *Royal Air Force Handbook 1939-1945* explains still further. It is a help to remember that a Training Unit operated within the Group it was intended to supply. So it is unlikely, on finding your man in a Squadron, that you will trace him back to a Training Unit outside his own Group or Command.

Always check the initials which follow a Commonwealth or Allied Squadron's number, and expect the Training Unit which supplied it to be generally (with obvious exceptions such as France and Poland) in that same country so No 10 Squadron could be one of four - RAF, RAAF, SAAF or RIAF. There is much more on this subject than this guide can reasonably cover - but the PRO indexes are comprehensive and self-explanatory.

OPERATIONS RECORD BOOK

A page from 247(F)(China British) Squadron's Operations Book on Form F540, as written up daily by an officer appointed to keep the record. In this case, by the Commanding Officer whose writing has not changed from that day to this. This is the summary of the month.

Page 15.

Date	Aircraft Type & Number	Crew	Duty	Time Up	Time Down	Details of Sortie or Flight	Reference
31.5.51	Meteor(?) VW.5	F. Watson		1520	1550		
	VW.5	Sgt Newcombe		1520	1550	Practice	
	VW.50	Murphy		1520	1550	"	
	VW.51	Main		1520	1550	"	
	VW.52	Wauchope		1520	1550	"	
31.5.51	W.953	Cruickshank		1610	1652	Target Practice	
	W.950	Flt Carver		1520	1520	"	
	W.954	Sgt Ross		1521	1565	"	
	W.951	Bower		1510	1520	"	
	W.950	Doherty		1535	1555	"	
	W.950	McKay		1710	1730	"	
	W.950	Abethyelt		1521	1555	Cloud Flying	
	W.900	—		1530	1555	Cloud Flying	
	W.950	Ross		1510	1540	Target Practice	
	W.957	Flt Carver		1510	1540	"	
	W.952	Sgt Dewitzer		1520	1520	Firing Practice	
	G.5051	Bowen		1520	902	"	
	W.950	Dewitzer		2055	2121	"	
	W.955	Flt Carver		1055	1055	Camera Gun	
	W.950	Sgt Doherty		1051	1520	Camera Gun	
	W.951	Abethyelt		1050	1525	Cine Firing	
	W.953	McKay		1055	1553	"	
	W.950	Dewitzer		1700	1720	Cine Gun	
	W.952	Flt Carver		1720	1730	"	
	W.952	Sgt Ross					

The daily record which shows the type of aircraft, pilot's name, up and down times, detail of sortie. This is a squadron of single seater fighters. A bomber crew will be entered in full with position in crew, rank and sometimes initials and number.

If the man or woman sought was in any way connected with aviation in Cumbria where a great many OTUs were based, or in the Dumfries and Galloway Regions, there are three books that will help. Parts 1, 2 & 3 of Peter Connon's *The Aeronautical History Of Cumbria* have already been published by St Patrick's Press, Penrith.

Records covered in AIR 28 and 29 are always a good starting point as they contain many American, Commonwealth, Polish and other Allied names. Information in these classes includes most of the main training stations. Often the Operations Books contain photographs of different groups as they passed through the various training courses at such places as Crosby on Eden (now Carlisle Airport), Cark, Windermere, Grange over Sands, Barrow in Furness, Millom, Silloth, Kirkbride, Great Orton, Kingstown, Carlisle, Wetherall, Longtown, Annan, Wigton, Wig Bay, West Freugh, Cargen House, Castle Kennedy, Corsewall, Stranraer, St Angelo and many more.

Any crashes in training are recorded in these ops books, and information has been collected and researched by local aviation recovery groups (details available from author). These give a man's number, rank, aircraft he was in, others with him and the circumstances. Resultant burials were often local and details may be found in the Commonwealth War Graves Commission's registers for the county. This is only one example of recovery and identification work being done all over the country.

Anyone serving in this area should contact Mr. Connon, via his publisher, with and for further information.

If it is a MOUNTAIN RESCUE TEAM you are researching, perhaps concerned with the above, your man is likely to be mentioned here too. They performed heroic actions often at the cost of their own lives, in conditions and at heights which only the experienced could endure. Many OTUs in the north, in Scotland and Wales, supposedly out of the reach of the enemy, were not. The mountains claimed their victims all too often. Cross reference the rescue team in MISCELLANEOUS UNITS, in AIR 29.

The injured and dead were brought back to the nearest RAF station, and in AIR 28/29 you may find them under STATION SICK QUARTERS (SSQ) with their parent bases notified. If not buried locally, but sent home for private burial, there is often reference to this which enables a further cross check with the CWGC. A copy of the CWGC index is at the IWM.

STATION SICK QUARTERS - SSQ

These are generally mentioned at the end of station records, not squadron records, in AIR 28/29. If your man or woman was a nursing orderly, medical assistant or a doctor, here is where you are likely to find the name. Most of the records give a general account of the state of health of the base, but if anything happened such as a fire or a crash, reference to those involved will be here. Some are mentioned by name. Staff and their postings-in or out are listed, usually with their service numbers. If the information is not here check the NOMINAL ROLL for nursing staff or try the Appendix books.

PHOTOGRAPHS as contained in OTUs, etc.

Service personnel were not supposed to take pictures of their base or aircraft. It is to our advantage that many disobeyed. Group photographs such as those contained here were official and therefore legal. They may not be copied and used without permission but most will yield a reasonable photocopy for private use. Official photographs are the principal evidence for the many batches of student navigators, engineers, pilots, etc taking courses. Many are annotated with names, course numbers, results, postings and subsequent fate. Information derived from this source can be used to determine which other records would be worth searching to fill in later career details. It should be noted that students with the same surname were often distinguished by the use of nicknames or the last three digits of their service number. In the context of photographs, uniform information is of help - eg dark blue for the Australian Air Force and badges of rank where plainly visible. OTUs organised by the RAF trained a wide variety of students including many from the RNAS (Royal Naval Air Service) and FAA (Fleet Air Arm). Test Pilots were on the staff, and here as well as at MUs, are many of their names. Also there are many of the ATA, both men and women, pilots and engineers, though not as part of the RAF.

PHOTOGRAPHS AT PRO, KEW

Aside from those already mentioned which may sometimes be found in OTU records, there is a file behind the enquiry desk in the main reference room which, though not yet complete, will refer you to photographs already known to be within other records. Ask for this, find the photos you need and put the class and piece numbers into the computer.

More are still being discovered by chance in other records but most, together with maps and descriptions of WWII airfields, are in AIR PUBLICATIONS - AIR 20/7585-6. Some in the Grantham area are in WORK 44. Photographs of airfields are in Air 10/4038-39.

Records of the Photographic Reconnaissance Units of the RAF (PRU) do not contain records of people. They were mainly for intelligence purposes and were taken while on bombing raids etc.

Official reconnaissance and bombing photographs are in various sections of the AIR class depending on what is being searched but these are not generally of use to the family historian. There may be some of the base and its people in the Appendix sections of AIR 27,28 and 29. If more on this subject is sought, those of the War in Western Europe are at the Air Photograph Library, Geography Department, University of Keele, Staffordshire ST5 5BG. There are many more at the IWM and at the RAF Museum, Hendon,as well as at smaller museums commemorating a particular RAF station such as Tangmere, West Sussex. In all cases it is advisable to telephone or write to say when you are coming.

For a search for a particular airman, the OTU course group records are the best. There are many examples, eg High Ercall 60 OTU is in AIR 29/684. Here there are sets of photographs, two to a page, of pilot groups and navigator groups, so it is not difficult to pair them up into crews. To many are added details of the squadron to which they were posted; to others their course results, and in some cases when/where they were reported missing or killed. Those who died are marked with an ink halo, though it is not possible now to know by whom they were thus marked. An invaluable goldmine if you recognise a face, your own crew or a name.

Having found the face/name you need, turn back to the rest of the book, find the corresponding course number under which will be further information.

Photocopies of such groups come out well, though when marking up the order slip, be sure to mention it is the photograph you want and a light exposure should be used. These can be done quickly and on the spot. A glossy photograph is better but takes longer and is more expensive - and may not be used without permission as it is the PRO's copyright. There is a leaflet explaining the costs and methods.

Similar material, but not details of courses etc, may be found in specialist magazines at the British Newspaper Library, Colindale Avenue, London NW9 5HE. Part of the British Library, it is in the same road as the RAF Museum at Hendon. Local newspapers too, may illustrate local heroes.

If any of this is being used for publication, copyright permission must be obtained. For personal use it is not required. It is also necessary if complete pages from the operations books are needed.

If, at this stage, you have written up the account of yourself, your crew or the person you are looking for, it would be a good idea to have copies made so that they may be deposited at the PRO, the RAF Museum or the Museum devoted to the squadron or station concerned - for posterity, not vanity.

PILOTS' LOGS, of which there are only a few at Kew, are found in AIR 4. These were the personal records of the hours flown, either under training, solo or on operations, by each pilot. Aircrew on bombers also kept a log. The entries include the type of aircraft; with whom he flew, if anyone; the aircraft number; second pilot or passenger; the duty; total hours flown at the end of each month and comment on each flight. Sometimes there will be personal remarks about what happened and to whom. Each is signed by his flight commander and his commanding officer so a few names of those with whom your man served are possible here. These other names and aircraft types lead to other records. For instance, usually at the back will be a list of aircraft your pilot is qualified to fly, and the aerodromes at which he has served and/or landed. Thus to find more about him, check these places in AIR 28 and 29.

The log remained the personal property of its owner and many are still in their owner's possession. Some have been donated to the PRO or to the RAF Museum by the pilot himself, or by his next of kin. These are an accurate way of finding out what happened when, as they were supposed to be kept up to date daily and countersigned, whereas other records were often made in retrospect. The logs of many famous pilots are at Kew.

There are a few personal Squadron Diaries and photographs which show how service people tried to keep a sense of balance and humour but these are not listed as such and if they survive will be in the Appendix sections. It is a matter of luck if they are found or if they survived, or even if there was time to keep such a diary in the first place. These are unofficial records and not to be confused with the Squadron Diary, the record of day to day duties. I was very lucky in finding the handwritten volumes kept by various members of 247(F), the squadron for which I was looking. Later I was able to identify the handwriting and the artist who had done many of the drawings. This was a squadron formed for the defence of Plymouth and Exeter in 1940, based at Portreath and Predannack in Cornwall. Many of the names mentioned have been traced, followed through and located, thus enabling the full story up to disbandment in 1957 to be written.

This is in AIR 27/1491 to 1494 on microfilm and in AIR 27/2482. I have not found anything similar for any other squadron, and would be pleased to know if anything comparable exists and for which squadron.

LOG BOOK of John Henry Bryant January 1944, 181 Sqn, whilst stationed at Odiham, Hants and Merston, Sussex, in the 2nd TAF. Later, CO of 247(F) Sqn, and known to them as Jimmy. Signed by F/Lt Ken Gear OC 'A' Flight, flight commander, 181 Sqn, 124 Wing, and by Sqn/Ldr James Keep OC 181 Sqn. Mentions loss of pilot Bud Allen. Flying Typhoons to which 247(F) had converted the year before at High Ercall, Salop (Shropshire).

TECHNICAL TRAINING - HALTON

At their main college, where most began whatever their rank now, technical airmen were known as "Halton Brats". Halton RAF College is, like the rest, found in AIR 29, but is broken down into various units and sections.

A technical airman is one who has served an apprenticeship as a fitter, rigger, armourer, mechanic or in one of the allied trades; in short, the non-flying ranks who kept the aircraft in the air so that the pilots could fly. You will need to know his entry number, otherwise it could be a long search but the Halton Aircraft Apprentices Association at RAF Halton, Buckinghamshire, may be able to advise.

Apprentices may be found in AIR 28/336-7 but the main search will be in AIR 29/713,717,727-8 and 757-9. The Works Squadron can be found in 826, the Station Flight in 940, the Hospital in 942, Medical in 1149, Tropical Medicine in 949 and the Cookery School in 1238 and many more.

Though these are usually the non-flying specialists, many have flying experience because armourers and fitters needed to accompany a pilot where possible to check their work. In latter years this has included women as there is now no sex discrimination in these ground trades. Many men thus trained also became pilots, and during the Battle of Britain many NCO pilots had come through this apprenticeship or were of the Volunteer Reserve.

The RAF Staff College at Andover is found in AIR 29/528 covering 1922 to 46. In some of its records there are useful photographs.

The RAF Regiment does not present as many difficulties as other non-flying ranks. If the number of the Regiment's squadron is known, AIR 29/100 is where to begin, but the names are elusive. Each posting and what happened there is listed. If the number is not known, it is advisable to look through a selection until the right area is found. There is an RAF Regiment Association.

Until January 1942 all the RAF's airfields and other units had been defended by the army (it is worth checking through RAF station records to find what these were), but for some time it had been under review whether they would be better served by a defence force of their own, releasing the army to its own tasks. The regiments thus formed were to be a Corps integrated within the RAF itself and in this way with a closer understanding of its needs and its procedures.

Major General Sir Claude Liardet was loaned by the Army to be its first Commander.

There were about 66,000 RAF personnel committed to defence. These were spread among 150 Defence Squadrons and 336 Defence Flights. The former, numbering 701 to 850, were renumbered as 2701 to 2850 and became the first official RAF Regiments. These will be found under their numbers in AIR 29 in the section so marked.

A Field Squadron (known as a Rifle Squadron) consisted of 7 officers and 170 airmen. Anti-Aircraft Flights had 1 officer and 60 men. These officers are often found in the records of the RAF station to which they are attached, their changes and replacements being noted. The Regiment fought in all the major landings and invasions as well as on the Home Front and in the Battle of Britain. For the Burma War a depot was established at Secunderabad.

Every RAF station had its own unit of the RAF Regiment, but they were not posted when and if the squadron was, instead they operated independently. AIR 28 and 29, therefore, gives the starting point for further information.

PRISONERS OF WAR

There are a great many records which deal with POW's. Some are better than others. AIR 20/3242 has an alphabetical list of 1944-45, but different camps may be listed separately. For example, Stalag Luft 7 is in AIR 40 but the infamous killing of 50 RAF officers in Stalag Luft 111 in Belavia is in AIR 2/10121.

In general, the army dealt with the camps via the Red Cross, so WO 165 and WO 208/3242 to 3566 and 3298 to 3327 may offer either what you need or lead to other lines of enquiry. (WO means a War Office Record). AIR 40/1897 names evaders and escapers by date and name. This latter is an invaluable document as it gives the full account as told by the man himself on returning to the UK or to Allied territory, often naming a great many more than that by which each file is headed. Each man was interrogated and the full story told in the special War Office room which was in the Great Central Hotel, Marylebone in 1945. In these notes you will sometimes find mention of a home address and the man's age. Usually in date order, these have an introductory index to each section and contain names from all three services. There are many very harrowing stories contained therein.

Some squadron records (AIR 27, Summary) note when one of their aircrew was reported as being taken prisoner. If he is named as missing, look further forward to see if this is so, and cross reference with WO 208 and AIR 40. PRO Leaflet 111 *Prisoners of War and Displaced Persons 1939-1953: Documents in the PRO* offers more piece numbers to be searched. AIR 1/892 has POWs in WWI.

PROMOTION of NCOs to Officers are contained in AIR 30/158 as well as those officers on probation who relinquished their commissions for one reason or another. This is unindexed and requires patience as it is listed in batches by date of recommendation.

AWARDS are in AIR 30/175 by year and also in AIR 2/9262. These should be cross referenced by date in the LONDON GAZETTE ZJ1/—, also in squadron records by date in AIR 27. An immediate award of the DFC or DFM usually means the man was dead or seriously injured. There is no comprehensive list of RAF medals as there is for the earlier Army medals but there are several specialists in this subject - ask at the main enquiry desk, first floor reference room. Today's RAF awards and promotions are usually made half yearly and can be checked in the indexes of newspapers like *The Times* and *Daily Telegraph*. These lists do not always give squadron numbers, but do give service numbers and rank. For NCOs and ORs not listed in the Air Force List in which the lowest rank mentioned is Warrant Officer, the London Gazette names all ranks being so awarded.

This is a printed publication found in ZJ1/- on the index shelves. It starts at a very early date and continues to the present day. The years up to and including WWII begin in the ZJ1/900 series and continue by year and month; the month ending the quarter ie March, June, September and December has the index for the quarter. Thus January 1940 is in ZJ1/932 and its index in March 1940 ZJ1/934.

Each book has about 800 pages, roughly one volume for each month so it is essential to note the page reference. All civilian and service awards, honours and promotions of officers are recorded here, some carry the citation and others much interesting detail. The services are divided into their respective sections but some names fall into more than one. Details can be cross-referenced in the Medal Roll microfiche for WWI RFC and with Squadron Records in AIR 27 for WWII. Squadron and service numbers are usually given, and all ranks are covered. To be listed here is the origin of to be *gazetted*.

INSTRUCTORS have already been referred to as possibly being listed in the records of the training units - OTU's etc. In addition, AIR 29/631 contains documents relating to the Flying Training Command Instructor's School at RAF Brize Norton and others. For Central Flying Training School - which was at no one place - look under that title in AIR 29 for the various piece numbers and also under the description of the unit and/or its name.

SUBMISSION PAPERS are in AIR 30. These are the papers relating to new commissions but they are not complete. They also list several permissions applied for by other non-British subjects wishing to join the pre-war RAF. As such they contain useful information, but require patient searching and definite starter clues. For example, Leslie Gordon Hill, American, 11 May 1937 is in AIR 30/197 and John Tansley, French citizen, is in AIR 30/199.

EXCHANGES OF USAAF AND UK RAF OFFICERS; AIR 20/7638 is an account of the suitability of selected RAF officers who were to be exchanged with their American counterparts to familiarise them with the equipment and methods of their respective countries. Here are some of the few personal notes we found. They state whether a man is married or not, his children and his age, but names of his family are not given. See also background data on the US 8th Air Force in the UK and material on the *Arnold* and *Tower* Training Schemes of UK aircrew in the USA.

USAAF:- there is not a great deal other than reports on raids and aerial combats by some - by no means all - American pilots based in the UK. AIR 50/343 is an account of USAAF Fighter Squadron 307, AIR 50/344 of 308 Squadron and AIR 50/345 of 309.

American pilots joining the RAF are in AIR 2/5163 - some of these may be traced via the OTU at which they are trained prior to 1942, for example at Upavon-Central Flying School AIR 29/604 1940, and at Annan 55 OTU 1940 to 43 in AIR 29/682 series.

Details of Deployment of USAAF Fighter Squadrons in the UK 1949- 50 are in AIR 16/1127, Fighter Groups in AIR 16/594-5 and Pursuit Groups in AIR 16/587-8. Others are in AIR 28/669 750-51 and AIR 8/797 718 1053 378, AIR 22/234 - 5 - 6 and others in these series.

The 8th Air Force Cemetery is at Maddingley, west of Cambridge. The American Air Force Museum is at Wright Patterson Field, Dayton, Ohio 4533 and the Centre for Air Force History is at Bolling AFB, Washington, USA.

Other useful piece numbers are AIR 40/349 - 1133: Air 14/2091: AIR 10/2814 and Air 20/7608 (which deals with the training of US Fighter Squadrons) and AIR 28/39. Check out these Air Class numbers in the index to see what they contain and if they are relevant to your search.

RAF Atcham's US squadrons are interesting in that the base was one of the first to be occupied by the 14th Fighter Wing and was known as Atcham Field in the American manner, although the RAF did not entirely abandon control. For a time it was the HQ and one of the busiest airfields in the Midlands, home to a wide variety of aircraft. Now it is a cabbage patch.

Centuries ago, when the Romans occupied Britain, just across the road which was the main runway at Atcham, lived the coincidentally named 14th Roman Legion, whose HQ was not far away at Wroxeter (equally bustling). Can it be reincarnation that the first pilot fatality of the 8th Air Force in Europe was here, and was First Lt.W.Giacomini (an Italian name) who crashed his Spitfire on approach?

USAAC (United States Army Air Corps) and USAAF or USAF are names for the same service. As with the RAF, the American Air Force began life attached to the Army. Later it gained independence as a service in its own right (known now as the USAF). The other two services retained their own air branches.

For further details on the 8th Air Force 2nd Air Division, read Martin Bowman's *The Fields Of Little America*, Patrick Stephens Ltd, 1977. This lists the bomber squadrons, their Groups and where they are stationed. Then cross reference the UK bases named with *Military Airfields In The British Isles* by Steve Willis and Barry Hollis, 1987. For example: The 578th Bomb Squadron, 392nd Bombardment group in 1943 was at Wendling in Norfolk which opened in 1941, closed in 1961, and had 421 officers and 2473 enlisted men.

FIELD MAPS

To flesh out the information discovered so far, maps and descriptions of airfields fill the environment in which the airman worked. These are found in AIR 10. To these maps are attached the physical details of dimensions, surrounding country, local flying hazards the length of runways etc. Compare these with modern maps to see what, if anything, remains. When visiting the area read the description in Halley's *Squadrons Of The RAF* and the *Action Stations* series.

For example: RAF ATCHAM, near Shrewsbury is found in AIR 10/4039, lying just off the Shrewsbury to Wellington road. The hangers and hard-standing parking bays are still there, as are the hazardous pylons described in the original description. It is difficult to visualise the Spitfires, Ansons, Masters, Fairchilds, Dominies, Lightnings and later Thunderbolts of the 307th US Fighter Group taking off and landing there. AIR 27 Operations Books give details.

AIR 28/39 tells of the airmen who died and were buried here in Atcham's parish churchyard, and describes their day to day existence. Examples of their aircraft can be seen in the RAF Museum at Hendon.

To expand all this still further, look at the local newspaper for 1941-1942 in the reference library at Shrewsbury and you will find a great deal to re-create Atcham as it was as well as many a service name that could have been based here. It was forbidden to mention the names of airfields, but it does not take much deduction to guess who played the first baseball match against the RAF.

Armed with this you can go to the County Record Office and find more of the background history especially of Attingham Park, where the unit's WAAFs were billeted, and the Mytton and Mermaid Hotel which was the Officers' Mess until their own was built. Very little of the airfield as such remains, but the perimeter track is still there though broken up, and there are a few brick gun emplacements.

AIRFIELD CONSTRUCTION UNITS are in AIR 29/826-7-8.

AIRFIELD BUILDINGS photos are in AIR 20/7585-6-7.

AIRCRAFT

There are photographs and references scattered through many records, but the AHB (Air Historical Branch of the Ministry of Defence) hold record cards which trace their history from factory to disposal and the RAF Museum is the best place of all to find examples. There are many books on the different types: *Hawker Hurricane* by Francis K Mason, Aston Books, 1987, lists the history of all the Hurricanes (by number and Mk) which he has traced so far. Other books deal similarly with the SPITFIRE and the MOSQUITO. There is also a HURRICANE ASSOCIATION, TYPHOON/TEMPEST ASSOCIATION, and the SPITFIRE SOCIETY. (sae or 3 IRCs to author for addresses.)

The Battle Of Britain Then And Now has a wealth of pictures of people, the aircraft in which they flew, their squadrons and their fate. From this book, which is available on the PRO's open shelves, it is possible to check, by date and squadron, more of your man's career in AIR 27.

THE VALUE OF SECONDARY SOURCES

SECONDARY SOURCES are those which are not the originals; generally printed material which can be found in repositories and libraries as well as at the PRO. Many of these sources have already been mentioned.

Since the 30 year secrecy rule was lifted in 1972 from reports of the Second World War, there has been a steady stream, sometimes a flood, of books, films, documentaries and TV series on the subject, a great many of them concerning the RAF, in fact and fiction. There is now no longer any need to accept that Errol Flynn won the war for most of the facts are available for anyone to look at and check their imagination by, as they were not when his films were made. Each year, in January, there is a new release of material, which, in the course of that year, will find its way into the AIR Class indexes, ie in 1989 the RAF records could be searched up to 1959.

This means that there are available a great many books on a great many subjects in public, specialist, lending and reference libraries. There are more in the non-lending copyright libraries, like the British Library (BL), to which publishers have to send a copy of any book put into print. The most elusive book can usually be borrowed via the LASER system at the local library, and some may be consulted at the PRO's own library.

If the local newspaper office itself does not have back copies, then most libraries have back copy files of their own local newspapers, otherwise these can be seen at Colindale Newspaper Library, at Hendon - a branch of the BL. These are the best sources for births, marriages and deaths during the war years, and activities of residents who have become service people are usually illustrated with a photograph. The names of air bases were suppressed for obvious security reasons, but it is not difficult to guess to which bases reports refer, especially if you know the area as it was in 1939-45. Some newspapers published a daily casualty list, as did the magazine *Flight*.

In the **Society of Genealogists** there is a series of scrap books of cuttings from the *Daily Telegraph*. These give births, marriages and deaths and IN MEMORIAM notices for the war years and are most useful as they give parents' names, wives' names and home town among other details.

The RAF itself publishes the *Royal Air Force News* fortnightly from the MoD at Turnstile House, 98 High Holborn, London WC1V 6LL. Mainly concerned with the modern airforce and presently serving personnel of all ranks, it includes reunion notices and 'help wanted' columns, as well as nostalgia pages and accounts of today's RAF stations. The editor will accept queries and "where are they now?" items. Keep requests as short as possible and give name, rank, number and place as well as date if known.

THE ROYAL AIR FORCE POCKET BOOK: the third edition of AP 1081, Air Publications, was published June 1937 by HMSO, and was for official use only. It was a pocket reference book used by non-specialist personnel who were operating away from their usual headquarters. Not meant as authority for action, nor as a textbook, but as guidance in discipline, the procedures for messages and signals, air navigation, liaison with the army and navy and much more, such as billetting, which may be obscure to the researcher.

Re-printed in February 1939, and again by NWR Printing Press, Moghalpura, India in 1942, they are worth looking for in second hand bookshops, particularly this edition as it covers the period of WWII.

THE RAF ASSOCIATION at 43 Grove Park Rd., Chiswick, London W4 3RU is for ex-RAF and WRAF people as well as present service members. It has local branches all over the country and publishes a quarterly magazine called *Air Mail*. This is an invaluable tool for the researcher as it covers much historical ground and runs columns of requests for those searching for old comrades. There are reunion announcements which may help you locate a man via his squadron association.

In many counties over the past few years there has grown up a series of air museums commemorating a station or a squadron, based on local interest. Many are on now-closed airfields such as TANGMERE, West Sussex, one of the best known fighter bases of the Battle of Britain. Most fighter squadrons were stationed there at some time during the period. There are museums that are part of an RAF complex, like the Yorkshire Air Museum, the runways of which are still used by nearby RAF stations. This is at ELVINGTON, near York, and seeks to commemorate 77 Squadron which was based there and the two Free French squadrons already commemorated by a memorial. Both these museums and others like them would welcome the results of your research and your help as they are staffed by volunteers. Elvington intends to re-create the huts and watch tower as they were in the hectic days when its CO, who still lives nearby, was the only air gunner to be given command of a squadron.

Contributory to and often part of these museums, in many counties where there was a concentration of airfields, are AVIATION RESEARCH AND RECOVERY GROUPS which set out to recover and record lost aircraft which crashed in their area. It is not possible for unauthorised people to go looking for wrecks as an MoD licence is needed. It **has to be remembered** that any that are found might possibly be graves and must not be disturbed without permission. Anything found must be notified to the authorities in the area. Details of these crashes can often be linked to squadron records and also to the Commonwealth War Graves Commission Registers as well as to the Air Historical Branch. Any information passed to any of these may result in a valuable gap filled for the personal researcher.

SQUADRON HISTORIES often appear in book form, well researched from PRO records and greatly added to by personal memories. A good example of this is *Under The White Rose*, the story of 609 SQUADRON, by its one-time intelligence officer Frank H Ziegler, MacDonald, 1971. Formerly the West Riding of Yorkshire Auxiliary Squadron (AAF) it was formed at Yeadon and composed of local Yorkshiremen but by 1944 its pilots were nearly all Belgian exiles. This is a well-illustrated book showing various aspects of the RAF Auxiliaries who fought in the Battle of Britain, with useful lists of names of members, many of whom have told their own stories such as Paul Richey's *Fighter Pilot* Batsford, 1955 and Jean Offenberg's *Lonely Warrior* Granada, 1969. An example of good cross-referencing may also be found here; Erik Haabjoern was in 609 Squadron as a F/Lt with the DFC. He became the Sqn/Ldr CO of 247(F) in August 1943. This immediately offers two sets of AIR 27 for research, as well as in the records of the Royal Norwegian Air Force and Foreign Office Files.

Detailed descriptions are also found in *Typhoon Pilot* by Desmond Scott who gives reasons for why so few nominal rolls are found in the ORBs, and explains the army co-operation. There is so much military overlap at this period of the 2nd TAF that you must be prepared to look at other than RAF/AIR records.

There were three types of TYPHOONS by now in the RAF - fighters, bombers and rocket-firing. Books about them can also be a help in locating which type your man flew or serviced. *Typhoon File* by Chris Thomas, son of a 247(F) Squadron Typhoon pilot, narrows the field, as does the bigger piece of research *The Typhoon And Tempest Story* by Chris Thomas and Christopher Shores, Arms and Armour Press.

As briefly mentioned, the 2nd TAF (TACTICAL AIR FORCE) was formed before, and for use in, the D Day invasion and should be looked for in the PRO under that title as well as under individual squadrons, wings and groups. After 1944 the ALLIED AIR FORCES IN EUROPE were merged under this one title. There is no room for detail here but an example suffices - 198 and 609 Squadrons, based at Manston in Kent, were the foundation of its 123 wing. Books on the subject after 1944 will, therefore, use the term 2nd TAF.

THE US 8TH AIR FORCE IN THE UK

Initially airfields occupied by the US Air Force were under RAF command and it must be remembered that most records will be in America. If looked for by the RAF name, the date of take-over can be found quite easily and the follow-through into the PRO's records located. Many such stations were at first shared by RAF and USAAF, the station commander was RAF and British.

The 8th AIR FORCE was formed on the 28th January 1942 at Hunter Field, Savannah, Georgia and commanded first by Col.Asa N Duncan, then by Major General Carl "Tooey" Spaatz. In England, at High Wycombe, it was commanded by Brigadier General Ira C Eaker and the HQ in Bushey Park, London, by Major General Spaatz. The first 8th Fighter op in WWII in Europe was on the 26th July 1942 and the first heavy bomber raid on 17th August the same year.

Van Haughland's *The Eagle Squadrons, Yanks in the RAF 1940-42* David and Charles 1979, is good introductory reading for American research queries. There are a few minor reference errors, however. At the PRO the first document for study should be AIR 28/669, 750 and 751, then AIR 8/979, 718 and 1053, and for training AIR 8/378. These cover the USAAC - United States Army Air Corps, as it was first called - in the UK in 1942.

AIR 40/411, AIR 14/2091 and AIR 10/3814 cover reports on raids in 1943. Other COMBAT REPORTS are in AIR 50, and in AIR 40/349 - 1133. The rest are all in the AIR class under US FORCES in the UK.

The contact HQ for the USAF HISTORICAL RESEARCH CENTER to obtain authorisation for access to information is AFOPA - MB, 1221 8th Fern Street, Arlington, VA 22202 USA.

The 8th USAAF occupied 112 airfields in Britain, eight were pre- war RAF stations, the rest built during the war. Most bomber stations were in East Anglia. Two books of help are *The Little Fields Of America* by Martin W Bowman, Patrick Stephens, 1977 and *The Bombers* by Robin Cross, Transworld Publishers Ltd, 1987.

It is essential to know in which Group of the 8th was the Wing sought - 1st, 2nd or 3rd Air Division - for example these wings were divided again into Groups - 2nd Combat Wing - 389th Bomb Group, 14th Combat Wing - 44th Bomb Group, 20th Combat Wing - 93rd Bomb Group and so on, all part of the 2nd Air Division. Each Group had at least four squadrons. Look at *Little Fields Of America* for clarification and an illustration of the Bomber Organisation Chart. Location of USAAC bases in the UK at the PRO can be found in AIR 22/324 1942-3, 22/325 1944, 22/326 1944-6. AIR 30/175 (Awards) includes a few USAAF commendations.

Badges of the 8th US Air Force

AMERICAN queries should be addressed to: **The Eighth Air Force Historical Society**, PO Box 3556, Hollywood, FL 33083 USA or **The Air Force Association**, Suite 400, 1750 Pennsylvania Ave NW, Washington DC 20006 USA which publishes a magazine similar to the RAF'S *Airmail* or:
The Retired Officer's Association, 201 N.Washington Street, Alexandria, VA 22314 USA.

The **Air Force Museum** is at Wright Paterson AFB, Dayton, Ohio, 45433 USA. There are others such as **HQ USAF Historical Research Center**, Maxwell Field, AL 36112-6678 USA.

The **American Cemetery** is at Maddingley, Cambridgeshire, once the heart of bomber country, and there are more graves in the military section of Brookwood Cemetery near Woking.

Norwich City Library has a 2nd Air Division Memorial Room for American airmen. (See also material on the *Arnold* and *Towers* Schemes.)

RAF **Duxford's Museum**, a branch of the IWM, has a permanent **8th Air Force Exhibition** in its collection of historical aircraft. The originals of these machines were first used for recognition training, being composed mainly of non-RAF machines, some having been captured from the enemy or crashed within the UK. They have been used in films and more recently, in TV reconstructions. RAF pilots ferrying machines of enemy origin during the war period did so under close fighter escort protection, for obvious reasons. See AIR 20/868, the Enemy Aircraft Units.

USAAF IN THE UK - The Eagle Squadrons

240 USA personnel enrolled as Eagles in the RAF 1939-41 including 37 who joined the RCAF. They were transferred to the USAAF in 1942. You will find them under their numbers in AIR 27.
　　Combat reports for the Eagles are in AIR 50/29 for 71 Sqn; AIR 50/45 for 121 Sqn and AIR 50/55 for 133 Sqn. General information on the USAAF in UK is found in AIR 22/324.
　　As the RFC became the RAF, so the USAAC became the USAAF and is now the USAF. There is a Naval Air Arm as there is a Fleet Air Arm.
　　Exchanges between RAF, USAAF and US Navy officers are also very useful for personal details. After the USA came into the war and in particular towards its end, in order to gain experience there was a detailed exchange between the different services of the Dominions, UK and USA. These will be found mainly in AIR 20/7638 and 6578-9.
　　An example from AIR 20/7638 is that of Fl.Lt.W.Cammell. He lived in No.37 Married Quarters at RAF Coltishall and went to the USA in August 1954 for attachment to the USAAF. He relieved F/Lt Gregory, already there, on 3200 Fighter Test Squadron at Eglin Air Force Base (abbreviated to AFB), Air Proving Ground, Florida. Cammell had been in the RNZAF flying ops in the UK on Lancasters with 115 Squadron. He was shot down in 1943 and became a POW in Germany. Returning, he was re-trained on jets and was of above average assessment. Described as enthusiastic, aged 31, married with two children, a boy aged 7 and a girl aged 4. He had approximately 1200 flying hours.
　　In reverse exchange, Capt Walter E.Domina USMC was posted to 41 Squadron RAF in June 1942. He described RAF Biggin Hill, which had been one of the main Battle of Britain stations for the defence of London, as being 'unsuitable as too near to London'. He said he had experienced the worst weather he had ever seen but the same 1940 spirit when Britain stood alone was still there.
　　From these examples, it will be seen that there are several good clues and research routes to follow.
　　The **Canadian War Museum**, 330 Sussex Drive, Ottawa, Ontario, Canada K1A OM8 has extensive and invaluable archive material on the **Canadian Air Force** and its people. There is a printed list of RCAF personnel on the open shelves at the PRO, bound in red, just beyond the RAF List which is bound in light blue.
　　There are many other museums and cemeteries of similar nature in allied and commonwealth countries. The CWGC may be referred to for cemeteries anywhere. For the FRENCH AIR FORCE and its members in the RAF, the **Service Historique de l'Armee de l'Air, Chateau de Vincennes (SHAA), 94300 Vincennes, France** has similar records.

OFFICIAL SOURCES AND ADDRESSES

Personal details of a man's or woman's service career, other than the final details of his conduct and death, may be obtained by writing to THE AIR HISTORICAL BRANCH (RAF), Ministry of Defence, Gt. Scotland Yard, Whitehall, London SW1A 2HW. This is a new library which also contains material for the other services but an appointment is required. Claims of medals and awards may also be obtained from RAF Innsworth (see below). Telephone for an appointment first if personal access to the library and records is desired. Name, rank and service number are required.

For the dead, next of kin only may be able to obtain details of a more personal nature from the following addresses -

Officers - RAF, PMC (AIR 1B), Eastern Avenue, Barnwood, Gloucester, GL3 E2.
Other Ranks - RAF P Man 3C(2) Innsworth, Gloucester GL3 E2.

If you are an ex-serviceman or woman, you may apply to these addresses for your own records. Again name, rank, number and last known station is needed. These Record Offices are the RAF's own, inherited from Ruislip and Uxbridge, which you will often find quoted in the F540s and F541s in the Operations Record Books. They may forward letters for enquirers to the last known civilian address. These Record Offices are **not** open to the public, and may be approached only by letter.

Failing this, there are many Squadron Associations, as well as the Aircrew Association, Guinea Pig Club, Caterpillar Club, Battle of Britain Association, The Arnold Register, and many more if you find your man was not a member of RAFA, the Royal Air Force Association, or the British Legion. Bear in mind there are people who do not want to belong to any of them. All these associations are run by volunteers so please enclose an sae or 3 IRCs.

If all this fails the author is compiling an INDEX OF RAF NAMES, culled from anywhere and everywhere, as well as from her own researches at the PRO. Its name, like this guide, is *How To Find The Few*. It began by being limited to aircrew but it was soon obvious that everyone must be included. Although there are now thousands of names in it, it is a lifetime's work and a long term project that cannot ever be completed as there will always be a new generation to add as well as names released by the 30 year rule. Parts of it have already been given, in rough form, to the RAF Museum at Hendon, its ultimate destination. By no means a comprehensive story of a persons life, it aims only to give searchers a starting point such as squadron number, a book reference or a newspaper announcement - such as the *Daily Telegraph* file or the Society of Genealogists, or any other clue that may give a lead. If you care to send any names you have, it will be appreciated and entered. A search may be made in it in return for an sae plus 2 first class stamps or 3 IRCs.

Births, marriages and deaths in the UK can, of course, still be looked up in the usual way, for a serviceman/woman, as for any other, at St. Catherine's House, 10 Kingsway, London WC2B 6JP, the Office of the Registrar General. See PRO Leaflet No.39 *Records of Births Marriages and Deaths*. But if the service man/woman died abroad, in whatever circumstances, or even off-shore UK, even though he/she were British, the name will not be here unless registered by the consul - see consular registers at the GRO. In the event of his being killed in action or on active service, the consular registration is not likely. There are however, indexes of wartime casualties available, though not necessarily complete. Look at the Runnymede Memorial for those of no known grave (some have been found later and rectified) or in the registers of the Commonwealth and Allied War Graves Commission - the CWGC - copies of which are in the IWM. Or in the RAF Chapel in Westminster Abbey, the RAF's own church of St.Clement Danes, London and the Rolls of Honour in Lincoln Cathedral.

If you do not know at least one of when, where or how, sadly there is not a great deal of hope of success.

FURTHER READING as quoted in text -

Portal Of Hungerford - Denis Richard, Heinemann 1977
*The Battle Of Britain, Then And Now** - After the Battle Publications
From The Ground Up and *From The Hangar Doors* - Fred Adkin,
Air Life Publications, Shrewsbury
*Squadrons Of The RAF** - James Halley, Air Britain Publications
*Roll Of Honour 115 SQDN**
*Air Force List**
*Fighter Squadrons Of The RAF** -   Rawlings, MacDonald 1964
*Bomber Squadrons Of The RAF**   Mayes, MacDonald 1964
History Of The Royal Air Force, Cranwell - Gp/Capt E B Haslam,
HMSO 1982
The Forgotten Pilots - Lettice Curtis, Nelson and Saunders 1971
Bomber Harris - Charles Messenger, Arms and Armour Press 1984
Mosquito Squadrons Of The RAF - Chaz Bowyer, Ian Allen 1984
Wings On Her Shoulder and *Partners in Blue* - Katherine Bentley Beaumont
The Enemy Is Listening - Aileen Clayton, Hutchinson 1980
Evidence In Camera - Constance Babbington-Smith, David and Charles 1957
Hawker Hurricane - Frank K Mason, Aston Publications 1987
Ribbons And Medals - H Tapprell Dorling, George Philip 1974
Fighter -Len Deighton, Panther 1979
The First And Last - Adolf Galland, Collins/Fontana 1970
The Narrow Margin - Derek Wood & Derek Dempster, Arrow/Hutchinson
The Bomber Command War Diaries - Martin Middlebrook & Chris Everitt
Viking 1985
The Aeronautical History Of Cumbria, Pts 1, 2 & 3 - Peter Cannon,
Penrith,St.Patrick's Press
The Fields Of Little America - Martin Bowmans, Patrick Stephens 1977
The Military Airfields In The British Isles -   Steve Willis and Barry Hollis
The Eagle Squadrons, Yanks in the RAF 1940-42 -Vern Haughland,
David & Charles 1987
Typhoon Pilot - Desmond Scott, Secker & Warburg 1982
Typhoon File - Chris Thomas
The Typhoon and Tempest Story - Chris Thomas and Christopher Shores
Under The White Rose, 609 SQUADRON - Frank Ziegler   MacDonald
Fighter Pilot - Paul Richard, Batsford 1955 (several editions,
first anonymously)
Lonely Warrior - Jean Offenburg, Granada 1969
The Bombers - Robin Cross, Transworld Publishers 1987

(* available on open shelves at the PRO)

There is a useful book of Military Abbreviations and another on the various code words used, such as OVERLORD, behind the main desk in the PRO main reference room.

Remember that the exact words of the author may not be quoted. These are protected by copyright and may not be used without his and his publisher's permission. There may be a reproduction fee to quote at length. Nor may photographs therein be reproduced in any way without similar permission or evidence that it has been sought. This is no idle statement at the beginning of the book. It is more than plagiarism to break copyright.

GENERAL BIBLIOGRAPHY

Action Stations - series published by Patrick Stephens, Wellingborough, Northamptonshire: illustrated with diagrams and photographs, explaining how to locate.
1. East Anglia
2. Lincolnshire
3. Wales & the North West
4. Yorkshire
5. South West
6. Cotswolds & Central Midlands
7. Scotland & North East and N.Ireland
8. Military Airfields of Greater London
9. Central and South East
10. Summary and Index

Fighter Command - Chaz Bowyer, J M Dent 1980
The Air War 1939-45 - R J Overy, Europa 1980
The Battle Of Britain - Len Deighton, Jonathan Cape 1980
The Bombers - Norman Longmate, Hutchinson 1983
Night Fighter - C F Rawnsley & Robert Wright, Collins 1957
Out Of The Blue - Laddie Lucas, Hutchinson 1958
The Last Enemy - Richard Hillary, MacMillan 1942
Coastal Command Leads The Invasion - Jarrolds
War In The Air - David Garnett, Chatto and Windus 1941
Fight For The Sky - Douglas Bader, Sidgwick & Jackson 1973
Piece Of Cake - Derek Robinson, Pan Books & Hamish Hamilton 1983
(filmed 1988 - fiction from fact)
Valedictory - W S Kiniczak
Airfields Of The 8th, Then And Now - Roger Freeman, After the Battle Publications
Fly And Deliver - Hugh Bergel, Air Life Ltd (about the ATA)
We Also Were There - "Archie" Hall, Merlin Books Devon (WAAFs)

There are too many to list them all, but many of these publishers have good book lists of their own, as have the various air publications such as FLY PAST, monthly and published from Key Publishing Ltd, PO Box 100, Stamford, Lincs PE9 1XQ: AIR MAIL, to which you can subscribe without being a member of the RAFA and RAF NEWS, an HMSO publication at Turnstile House, 98 High Holborn, London WC1V 8LL.

In preparation and to be published by an American publisher - the author's own bibliography of the Battle of Britain. It will be on sale here. Another is in preparation about the RAF in general.

SPECIALIST SUPPLIERS

There are many specialist bookshops, some of which put out mail order lists selling new and secondhand books on flying. Too many RAF books are now out of print and the secondhand market is often the only way of finding them. Try **Midland Publications**, 3 Land Society Lane, A47, Earl Shilton, Leicester LE9 7NA. Their warehouse is a joy to bookworms.

Terry Smith Balwyn House, The Common, Freethorpe, Norwich NR13 3LX - ask for the aviation list.

Falconwood Transport & Military Bookshop, 5 Falconwood Parade, The Green, Welling, Kent DA16 2PL

Vintage Aviation Books, 56 Ravensheugh Rd, Musselburgh.

Ray Roberts, Whiston Hall, Penkridge, Staffordshire ST19 5QH

Motor Books 33 (FP) has several branches; the London one is at St Martin's Court, WC2N 4AL.

Pickerings in the Shambles, York, which is closely connected with the Yorkshire Air Museum at nearby Elvington.

And of course the shop in the **RAF Museum at Hendon**.

There are publishers also who have a specialist department, **Putnams and William Kimber** are but two.

There is, of course, a great deal more and every PRO file is full of surprises, even to the initiated, but, as they say, one thing (PRO class references) leads to another.

Take heart - there was an unwritten motto fighter pilots swore by -
"He who flies high with his back to the sun, sees the enemy first and lives out the day".

ABBREVIATIONS, INITIALS and COMMON USAGE SLANG - as used in text

AAF	-	Australian Air Force
AC1 and AC2	-	Aircraftman first and second class - ACW, aircraftwoman
Ack Ack	-	Anti aircraft fire, or AA, - flak
ACM	-	Air Chief Marshall
ADM	-	Admiralty
AMES	-	Air Ministry Experimental Station
ATA	-	Air Transport Auxiliary (civilians)
ATC	-	Air Training Corps and Air Traffic Control
Aux AF	-	Auxiliary Air Force
AVM	-	Air Vice Marshall
A/c	-	Aircraft
a/g	-	air gunner
BAFF	-	British Air Forces in France
BL	-	British Library
CB	-	confined to barracks
CU	-	Conversion Unit - training on another type of aircraft
CWGC	-	Commonwealth War Graves Commission
EFTS	-	Elementary Flying Training School
GAF	-	German Air Force
GC & CS	-	Government Code and Cypher School
glasshouse	-	prison on camp
HCU	-	Heavy Conversion Unit - heavy bombers
HMSO	-	Her Majesty's Stationery Office
IAF	-	Italian Air Force
IRC	-	International Reply Coupon
ITW	-	Initial Training Wing
IWM	-	Imperial War Museum
Jankers	-	punishment parade
mug	-	mid upper gunner
nav	-	navigator
NCO	-	non-commissioned officer
ORBs	-	operation books
OTU	-	Operational Training Unit
PDU	-	Photographic Development Unit
PIU	-	Photo Intelligence Unit
PR	-	Photographic reconnaissance - PRU - unit
PRO	-	Public Record Office
RAF	-	Royal Air Force
RAFO	-	Reserve of Air Force Officers
RAFVR	-	Royal Air Force Volunteer Reserve
r/g	-	rear gunner
r/t	-	radio telegraphy
SFTS	-	Service Flying Training School
SRO	-	station routine orders
SWO	-	Station Warrant Officer
Sqn Ldr	-	Squadron Leader
sae	-	stamped addressed envelope
WO	-	War Office
wop/ag	-	wireless operator/air gunner
w/e/f	-	with effect from
W/O	-	Warrant Officer
WWI/II	-	World War I and World War II
Y	-	interpretation of signals